THE LAYMAN'S BIBLE COMMENTARY

THE LAYMAN'S BIBLE COMMENTARY
IN TWENTY-FIVE VOLUMES

THE LAYMAN'S
BIBLE COMMENTARY

Balmer H. Kelly, *Editor*

Donald G. Miller   *Associate Editors*   Arnold B. Rhodes

Dwight M. Chalmers, *Editor, John Knox Press*

VOLUME 10

THE PROVERBS

ECCLESIASTES

THE SONG OF SOLOMON

J. Coert Rylaarsdam

JOHN KNOX PRESS
Atlanta

Published in Great Britain by SCM Press Ltd., London.

Fifth printing 1976

Complete: ISBN: 0–8042–3026–9

This volume: 0–8042–3010–2

Library of Congress Catalog Card Number: 59–10454

Printed in the United States of America

PREFACE

The LAYMAN'S BIBLE COMMENTARY is based on the conviction that the Bible has the Word of good news for the whole world. The Bible is not the property of a special group. It is not even the property and concern of the Church alone. It is given to the Church for its own life but also to bring God's offer of life to all mankind—wherever there are ears to hear and hearts to respond.

It is this point of view which binds the separate parts of the LAYMAN'S BIBLE COMMENTARY into a unity. There are many volumes and many writers, coming from varied backgrounds, as is the case with the Bible itself. But also as with the Bible there is a unity of purpose and of faith. The purpose is to clarify the situations and language of the Bible that it may be more and more fully understood. The faith is that in the Bible there is essentially one Word, one message of salvation, one gospel.

The LAYMAN'S BIBLE COMMENTARY is designed to be a concise, non-technical guide for the layman in personal study of his own Bible. Therefore, no biblical text is printed along with the comment upon it. This commentary will have done its work precisely to the degree in which it moves its readers to take up the Bible for themselves.

The writers have used the Revised Standard Version of the Bible as their basic text. Occasionally they have differed from this translation. Where this is the case they have given their reasons. In the main, no attempt has been made either to justify the wording of the Revised Standard Version or to compare it with other translations.

The objective in this commentary is to provide the most helpful explanation of fundamental matters in simple, up-to-date terms. Exhaustive treatment of subjects has not been undertaken.

In our age knowledge of the Bible is perilously low. At the same time there are signs that many people are longing for help in getting such knowledge. Knowledge of and about the Bible is, of course, not enough. The grace of God and the work of the Holy Spirit are essential to the renewal of life through the Scriptures. It is in the happy confidence that the great hunger for the Word is a sign of God's grace already operating within men, and that the Spirit works most wonderfully where the Word is familiarly known, that this commentary has been written and published.

THE EDITORS AND
THE PUBLISHERS

THE PROVERBS

Setting

The Book of Proverbs is the oldest written product of the wisdom movement in Israel. Other writings of this movement include Job and Ecclesiastes in the Hebrew canon and the books of Ecclesiasticus (the Wisdom of Jesus the Son of Sirach) and the Wisdom of Solomon in the Apocrypha. Several Psalms (for example, 1, 49, 127) also constitute writings of the wisdom movement, as does a section of the Book of Baruch (3:9—4:4) in the Apocrypha. In the New Testament the parables in the Synoptic Gospels and the Epistle of James show considerable literary dependence on this literature; in Judaism it lives on in the Sayings of the Fathers (*Pirke Aboth*) as well as in the rabbinic materials generally.

King Solomon was probably the official founder of Israel's wisdom movement, and he continued to serve as its patron. His was a great period in the national history. Foreign influences of all sorts—in art and architecture, in social and political administration, in commercial organization, in religion and worship, and in court life—came into the country under Solomon's sponsorship and were adapted to Israel's traditions and situation, often being assimilated and becoming a part of these. The rise of the wisdom movement owed a great deal to this general development. The close cultural and political ties between Solomon and Egypt are also reflected in the close connection between Israel's wisdom movement and that of Egypt, which is demonstrable in terms of actual literary dependence, as well as in the general tone and function of both.

The voluminous wisdom literature of Egypt, much of it reaching far back into the third millennium B.C., and some of it contemporary with Proverbs, has greatly illumined our understanding of the background and setting for Israel's wisdom. The movement flourished in the circles of the royal court; it expressed itself as an educational activity of sages or teachers who undertook the responsibility of training the sons of the nobility and preparing them to exercise the roles of leadership and rule for which their station intended them. It seems almost certain that the Book of Proverbs was the outcome of an analogous context in Jerusalem during the period of the monarchy. First Kings 4:29-34 credits Solomon himself with taking the lead in this educational function, crediting him with proverbs, songs, and fables. In Proverbs 25:1 the heading to a large collection of proverbs describes them as having been "copied" by the men of King Hezekiah of Judah, reflecting the permanence of the movement at the court. In Egypt the copying of proverbs from older sources was part of the training of the pupils of the sages. This was probably increasingly true in Israel also, though the initial pronouncement of proverbs by the wise was oral. Proverbs, like the Egyptian wisdom literature to which it corresponds most closely, combines the attempt to tell the truth about man's existence with the concern to perform a very practical and useful educational function. In both we detect an aristocratic, class-conscious, conservative attitude toward life and society, coupled with an intense sense of responsibility and *noblesse oblige*. In Israel the movement was gradually penetrated by the distinctive features of her election faith, but in the Book of Proverbs this process has barely begun.

Literary Analysis and Data

The basic literary unit in the book is the *māshāl*, literally, the comparison or parable, consisting of two parallel lines. The relation between the lines may be antithetical or synonymous. Each such couplet makes a single point. The idea that this literary style had its origin in an oracular cultic pronouncement can be argued persuasively. But it must be added that in Proverbs it is then far removed from its original setting. Here its function is to serve as a concise and arresting vehicle for strictly rational and clear-cut human insights.

The long section with the title "The proverbs of Solomon" (10:1—22:16) consists almost exclusively of such couplets. This is the chief reason for considering it the oldest part of the book. Gradually this basic literary form was expanded and/or mixed with other forms; for example, 1:20-33 shows influences of the prophetic oracle, and the numerical sayings in chapter 30 are derived from a popular form of the riddle. In the section from

22:17 to 24:22 an Israelite sage copied the style as well as some of the contents of an Egyptian wisdom document. The result of these developments was that in its later stages the movement's work consists of longer and more varied units: discourses, essays, and stories. The New Testament parables in the form of stories are one example of such expansion of the *māshāl* form.

From what has been said it will be clear that the Book of Proverbs is not a document that can be assigned to a specific date. It is the outcome of a process of thought and work that continued for centuries, and in which writing was a by-product of oral teaching. It is also very probable that many materials in the book appeared in earlier documents that were displaced or changed in the production of the documents that finally went into the making of the present Book of Proverbs. That several separate documents are imbedded in the book seems clear both from the variations in style and from the content of the headings of some of its sections. But it is not possible to say absolutely whether or to what extent the editor who combined them all added to or altered any of them. It appears that such additions were very limited in all sections, with the exception of the first. And with respect to the first it seems possible to entertain the view that its author could also have been the collector and editor of the book as a whole.

The exilic or early postexilic period seems to be the most plausible setting for the composition of the first, and youngest, section, chapters 1-9. Its affinities with Isaiah 40-55 weigh heavily in this judgment. Then, if the author of this section was also the editor of the book, we could say that the "date" of Proverbs is from the middle of the tenth century (Solomon) to the middle of the sixth, with the completion of the work at that point. It may have been quite a bit later, however. The Wisdom of Jesus Son of Sirach, written about 180 B.C., shows us that by that time Proverbs had a solid place in Israel's literary and religious tradition.

The Purpose of the Book and Its Message

The purpose of the wisdom movement was initially a very practical one: to educate the nobility for cultural and political leadership. The wise men were teachers whose main concern was to inform and discipline the mind and life of youth at an impressionable moment. They probably joined forces with the scribes or court secretaries (Ps. 45:1) for the literary side of their work.

In Israel, however, this practical purpose of the movement is increasingly matched by a concern to say in human terms what the ultimate meaning of man's life is: what its real goal is, how this is to be attained, and by what means. In modern terms, from being a movement concerned with practical ethics it becomes a movement increasingly concerned with religious and theological issues. In this respect Israel's wisdom movement developed much further than that of Egypt or of other Near Eastern cultures; and its distinctiveness is bound up with this development. Though the development is no doubt impelled by Israel's election faith, with its confession of historical revelation, the familiar themes of this faith do not become explicit in the Book of Proverbs. That happens later in the history of the wisdom movement and is documented in the Wisdom of Jesus ben Sirach and in the Wisdom of Solomon. Consequently, Proverbs differs markedly from most of the rest of the Old Testament.

Proverbs is different, first of all, because of its emphasis on man's search. The Bible as a whole is God-centered; it looks at man's life in terms of what God has done, does, and plans to do, so that it reads like a history of the acts of God. Further, often, as in the prophets, this God-centeredness of the Bible is emphasized by the fact that the men who produced it speak and write in the name of God. They are not men talking about God, or seeking to discover him; they are men to whom God has come and who are seeking to respond to him or to bear witness to him. In Proverbs the authors seek to discover God. Reason, experience, thought, and even elementary science are the means of their quest. In this respect the book is close to the spirit of modern man. Some parts of Proverbs tend to take a static view of God; it comes close to equating "the LORD," its favorite name for him, with what we would call "the moral law of the universe." And all the study of its writers is designed to discover and describe this moral law in a way that will make it serve as a practical guide for life. The teachings of the wise are a law of life; but, unlike the Law of Moses, they are not an outright gift of God but a truth to be discovered. The emphasis falls on man's responsibility rather than on the redeeming action of God. It must be noted, however, that in the youngest section of the book (chs. 1-9) there is a growing awareness of the universal initiative of God by which he prompts men to seek him. But this prompting occurs in and by the order of creation, rather than in the specific events of redemption.

A second distinctive feature of Proverbs, in which it differs from the Bible as a whole, is derivative from the first: it ignores the history of Israel. Such topics as the patriarchs and the covenant with Abraham, the Exodus and the Covenant of Sinai, the wilderness wandering and the Conquest, or even the establishment of throne and Temple are ignored. Why? Elsewhere these themes were important because they represented God's special revelation of himself in Israel's history, his redemption and election of his people. But since, as noted, the sages in Proverbs do not think of an action of God in this particular manner, these topics have no role to play for them. Only later, when sages like Jesus ben Sirach equate the man-centered and man-discovered wisdom of the sages with the Law given on Sinai can this whole particular tradition of Israel's faith begin to function again in the wisdom literature. There was no tension between reason and revelation because revelation came by reason.

A third distinctive feature about Proverbs is its optimism about the possibility of achieving the goal of life. God has so made man that he can discover the truth about the moral and natural law by which his life is controlled and thus can obtain the reward that comes with obedience to it. There remains a mystery about God and his ways, but it is not so great as to make man's quest hopeless. This, with minor exceptions (see 30:1-4), is the view of Proverbs. It differs in this from such other wisdom books as Job and Ecclesiastes, which, for different reasons, despair of the human quest.

O U T L I N E

COMMENTARY

THE TITLE
Proverbs 1:1

The Book of Proverbs as we now have it contains several
collections of sayings. Each had its own history and function.
But the general subject matter and concern of all are similar.
Hence they were combined in a single book which can be thought
of as "An Anthology of Israelite Wisdom." This verse is probably
the title for the entire book, not only for the first section of it.
The Hebrew word for "proverb" literally means "simile"; two
things or persons are compared to one another, whether in similarity or in contrast. The parables of Jesus in the New Testament
are a continuation of the same form of teaching.

The king was a mysterious figure in the ancient Near East,
one who by virtue of his status was thought to have special
access to divine knowledge and to be the one through whom
some of this knowledge was communicated to men. There is
evidence in the Old Testament that some of these notions about
the king were also very prevalent in Israel, especially with respect to the royal house of David. The wise sayings of this book
are called "proverbs of Solomon." This is done, first of all,
because Solomon was indeed a man of great sagacity and judgment (I Kings 3:12, 16-28), who founded the wisdom movement
in Israel (I Kings 4:29-34); and it can be assumed that at least
some of the proverbs in this book actually originated with him.
But it may also be that the designation is intended to intimate
that the wisdom of the proverbs, which is so largely the outcome
of man's evaluation of the common experiences of life, is not
just a human thing but is an expression of divine truth as well.

FIRST SECTION: DISCOURSES ON WISDOM
Proverbs 1:2—9:18

The Purpose of Proverbs (1:2-6)

The purpose of the literature is educational; by the pondering
of these proverbs men will be formed in sagacity and self-discipline. They are not simply to commit these sayings to memory,

though that was no doubt expected; they are to absorb their implications for their own lives. The word "instruction" includes the idea of discipline and training. It is not enough simply to be committed to "righteousness, justice, and equity." One must know how to decide what action this commitment calls for in specific cases. The wisdom movement in Israel stood for calm and rational treatment of every social and ethical situation. Cool, disinterested judgment rather than the indulgence of the emotions was its ideal for every man.

The book is first of all for the inexperienced and the young, to build character and standards of conduct. But there is something in it for everybody and for all stages of life. In the Church we say that Scripture has a message for the lettered and the unlettered; it is the instrument that awakens and nurtures our faith in God. So this statement of purpose assumes that the proverbs are an inexhaustible resource for growth in character and personal understanding; even a sage can hear them again to his profit. For the sages of Israel's wisdom movement, Scripture is "classic" in the sense that it lives for every successive generation because it has something important to say to each. At the same time, it is the Word of God in which God's action and purpose are revealed. Christians must learn to understand this close correlation of the specifically religious with the cultural resources in Judaism; it is most conspicuous in the wisdom movement.

Christians vary greatly in the value they attach to "religious education" as the religious nurture of youth through the transmission of the cultic and cultural legacy of faith. Some hold that this is the means by which the Holy Spirit does his work of awakening a personal religious consciousness which issues in a confession of faith and a maintenance of it; others come close to the view that it is a barrier to the Holy Spirit. It is clear that a book such as Proverbs holds the former view; moreover, it pursues that view more exclusively and single-mindedly than any Christian group.

The Motto of the Movement (1:7)

This motto is shaped by the parallelistic structure characteristic of all Hebrew poetry, and notably of Proverbs. The parallelism in this verse is antithetic; that is, the second line clarifies the first by describing its opposite. "Wisdom and instruction" quicken "the fear of the LORD"; conversely, this "fear" moves men to seek instruction and wisdom. Fools are people who take seriously neither God nor learning. To fear God is not to be afraid of him but to stand in awe of him, because the meaning of everything and the destiny of every person are determined by what God is and does. The wise man is one who has a living awareness of this centrality of God in all things and an insight into the character of his rule (see 9:10). The term for "beginning" as used here includes such meanings as "starting point" and "chief part"; it is not to be understood only in chronological terms. The fear of God is itself the very heart of knowledge. The basic relation of God as Creator and man as his creature both prompts and governs man's quest for wisdom. The fools (literally "fat ones") are a class opposite to the wise (10:14; 11:29; 12:15-16); in despising study they despise their Creator.

The Parable of the Racketeer (1:8-19)

The racketeer is a person who is ready to break whatever laws he must break to obtain what he wants. His lust for goods or power decides his whole course of action. If chicanery will not suffice, he will turn to robbery and murder. He gets "gain by violence" (vs. 19). Next to the idolatry of apostates to Baal this is the behavior most frequently and severely condemned in Israel. Frequently, as by the prophet Hosea, idolatry and "violence" are associated with each other.

The main point of this parable is that the racketeer destroys himself (vs. 19). The man of "violence" denies God and his moral rule. He scoffs at the rights of his fellow men under this rule. He is one example of the fool who does not take God into account. Sometimes the racketeer loses his physical life; sometimes he forfeits his capacity for living.

A note of wry humor is introduced at the close of the picture, to point up the stupidity of the racketeer. A hunter would not spread a net in sight of the bird he wants to catch. The bird would avoid it. But the foolish man of violence sets the trap for his own life (vss. 17-18).

The author's example of the racketeer seems to be that of a man who joins a gang of highway bandits. Such bandits were common in all biblical history (Judges 5:6; Luke 10:30). The mountainous character of much of the terrain in the Holy Land and the frequent breakdown of central political power facilitated the bandits' operations. They are sketched here in vivid strokes: they lie in ambush to murder unsuspecting merchant travelers, like the bands that rob the stagecoach in an American "Western"; they "have one purse" (vs. 14).

The sage tells his pupils ("my son" was a form of address used by a teacher) that the traditions about man's way of life in "the fear of the LORD" are the best antidote to the lure of the life of violence. The interpretation of these traditions will provide the young with an informed and reasonable "no" to temptation.

This parable reminds us that there are many echoes of Proverbs in the sayings of Jesus. It can be summed up in the words "What will it profit a man, if he gains the whole world and forfeits his life?" (Matt. 16:26). The parable of the Rich Fool (Luke 12:16-21) makes precisely the same point as this one of the Racketeer, even though the rich fool is a law-abiding citizen, full of civic virtue! The fool is one who thinks there are substitutes for the security of God.

Wisdom's Call to Repentance (1:20-33)

In Proverbs the word "wisdom" usually refers to the cultural materials or resources that are available for the educational task: the lore of ancient traditions, whether in written or oral forms; the discipline of parents and the standards of domestic and social life; and, especially, the understanding of sages whose special function it is to teach and interpret all of these things. Wisdom is a common noun, designating an impersonal item or quality. Here, we have an exception. Wisdom here is a person, a preacher issuing a call to repentance. Similar examples of a personified wisdom are found in chapters 8 and 9. In the later writings of the Jewish wisdom movement the personification of Wisdom is increasingly common; the fact that in Proverbs it is limited to chapters 1-9 therefore tends to support the view that this is the youngest section of the book.

Whenever Wisdom is personified it is either as a divine messenger or spokesman or as a divine being. Here she assumes the role of a prophet appointed by God. There is an urgency about her mission. As the great prophets of Israel, she goes to the people, to the market place and to the city gate. And, like Habakkuk (Hab. 2:1), she assumes the role of a watchman on the wall. She raises her voice, issues a loud cry, calls for attention and speaks (vss. 20-21), taking on the rough-and-tumble role of a prophetic street preacher.

If one studies Proverbs carefully he must conclude that there was a prevalent view that the likelihood of a change of heart in the foolish or wicked was slight. Often those who pursue wisdom or righteousness are told to shun such persons and avoid wasting their time or becoming contaminated. The note of what is sometimes called predestination is quite strong in the wisdom movement. Nevertheless, God, through the prophetic Wisdom, issues his call to these unpromising prospects. The term translated "give heed" in verse 23 literally means "turn," the technical Hebrew word for "repent." What is more, this call to repentance is accompanied by a promise which can be translated: "I will cause my spirit to pour out upon you . . . make my words known to you." But this redeeming and healing action of God through Wisdom cannot take place until those addressed sense their need and "turn." And it is typical of the simple and the foolish that they do not sense their need.

Wisdom, we see, offers her "spirit" and her "words" (vs. 23, see margin). In later stages of the wisdom movement the personified Wisdom is synonymous with the Spirit of God, with the Word of God, and with the Law of God. In the New Testament Jesus Christ is, consequently, designated Spirit (II Cor. 3:18), Word (John 1:14), and Wisdom (I Cor. 1:24).

Those who heed the call to repentance enter on the path to life (vs. 33); those who ignore it are on the way to death (vs. 32). Men cannot live without the grace and help of God, but they are responsible for their own destruction. This section emphasizes that there is a season for grace and for entering upon the way of Wisdom. Once the choice has been made it cannot be undone. The road taken must be followed to the end. In prophetic fashion this text makes the daring statement that Wisdom (that is, God, acting in her) laughs and sneers at those who have rejected her when they panic upon discovering their fate. In verse 28 the Hebrew word for "Then" in the prophetic vocabulary refers to the decisive moment when at the "last day" men will call upon God but he "will not answer." They will seek for the divine Wisdom that once appealed to them, but she will not be found. The doctrine of the "two ways," very familiar in some later stages of Judaism, and also adopted in Christian preaching, had its beginning in a call to repentance such as this, with its emphasis upon the consequences of rejection. In the Sermon on the Mount the same theme is beautifully presented in the parable of the Houses, one built on rock, the other on sand (Matt. 7:24-27).

It is important to consider the nature of the relation between this Wisdom as a personification of the activity of God and the "wisdom" that made up the lore and understanding of the sages. It is not easy to be clear about this relation in every respect. Wisdom as a human possession was a product of human experience, sharpened and ordered by analysis and reason. It was the product and means of what we call education, the result and instrument of man's self-understanding. Israel's wisdom movement represented the whole range of social and humanistic concerns. In Proverbs, wisdom is not a special gift of grace to Israel such as the Law, for example; it lies in the universal order of nature and creation. In introducing a personified divine Wisdom that represented the initiative of God in seeking, calling, and instructing men, the sages seem to have sought to convey their belief that God acted in, through, and by means of their movement to reveal himself to men. It is not unimportant to notice in this connection that in Proverbs we have no reference to God's special disclosure of himself to Israel as represented by the history beginning with the Exodus and by the Covenant and the Law. Nor is there any interest in the cultus with its festivals and rites that were based on this revelation. The divine Wisdom here connotes an active God, living and working out his purpose in the cultural enterprise of people dedicated to seeking the true and the good. He is not a God breaking into the order of things at a special point or in a particular event, but is immanent in it.

Five Rewards of Wisdom (2:1-22)

This chapter is a unit by itself. It is a poetic essay in which a sage addresses his pupil. He urges him, with overtones of deep emotion, to commit himself heart and soul to seek wisdom and itemizes five results that will follow. Artistically the poem consists of a protasis or condition (vss. 1-4) with a fivefold conclusion (vss. 5-8, 9-11, 12-15, 16-19, 20-22).

What strikes one most forcibly about the call issued in the

first four verses is the quality of urgency that pervades it. The
search for wisdom was formally similar to what we call education, but in these verses the success of this search is a life or
death matter. It calls for the dedication of one's whole being. In
many parts of the Old Testament we meet such urgency in
respect to the words of the Law. Morning and evening, at home
and abroad, one must keep its words at the focus of one's attention (Deut. 6:1-9). They should be written on one's heart
(Jer. 31:33). That is precisely the sort of wholehearted urgency
that is invoked here. Such single-mindedness is first of all
evident in the formal deportment of the student. He masters
what the sage gives him (vs. 1). He leans forward to get every
word and shows that he takes it seriously (vs. 2). But if the
quest is to succeed there must be something more personal, something that lasts twenty-four hours a day and does not need or
depend on the sage or the classroom: the cry for understanding.
The quest must become a prayer, an anguished call for light
(vs. 3). We must remember that for the sages, God disclosed
himself by means of this educational process; it was not simply
a practical device by which one became a respectable member
of society or qualified for a profession. Study and prayer were
inseparable. Hence the "if" of verse 1 leads to the "yes, if" of
verse 3; and in verse 4 we return to the simple "if," the plodding
search in which the pupil spares no effort and finds no burden
too great.

The urgent call to full dedication is matched by buoyant
confidence. To be sure, the substance of this buoyancy is provided in the results that are to follow. But the spirit of it
pervades the statement of the condition; one senses that the
search will bear fruit: ". . . if you seek it like silver . . ." The
implication is, "You will find it." In contrast to Job 28, which
tells us that man can discover the precious silver in the mine but
that he cannot discover "wisdom," this poet assumes that God
responds to man's quest and prayer by revealing his ways to
him. He assumes an availability and comprehensibility of revelation that is questioned by Job and Ecclesiastes.

The aura of hope and confidence pervading the call is made
concrete in the results that come to those who respond to it.
The first reward (vss. 5-8) of the man who perseveres is that he
will "find the knowledge of God." The "fear" of God, the
"knowledge" of him, and wisdom are all synonyms. The wise
man takes God seriously; he orders his life on the assumption

that God, and not he himself, is at the center. The wise man
"knows" God; that is, he is acquainted with him. He knows what
God will do for him and what he expects of him. That is wisdom.

The poet is certain that the faithful quest will issue in knowledge of God because "the LORD gives wisdom" (vs. 6). God, for
him, is not simply a static form, a structure of laws and principles
to be discovered. As in 1:20-33, he is the active, seeking God
who comes to men who open their hearts to him. Man can
discover wisdom because God "stores up sound wisdom" to give
to him, and because he protects those who put their trust in him.

The next great reward that comes to those who are faithful
in the single-minded quest for wisdom is that it gives understanding and freedom (vss. 9-12). Man will know how to decide
what constitutes "righteousness and justice" in concrete situations. A man's ability to choose a "good path" was due to the
security and freedom that came to him by virtue of his "knowledge" of God as much as to his mastery of the lore he was
taught. The faithful quest and the action of God in relation to
it integrated his life; he became a whole person. Desire and duty
began to coalesce. Wisdom informed his mind ("heart"), and
the whole personality ("soul") found knowledge attractive (vs.
10).

The first two rewards coming to those who persevere in the
quest for wisdom were introduced by a decisive "Then" (vss.
5, 9). The three that now follow are really only corollaries of
those two. Blessed with a knowledge of God and with wholeness
of life, the sage is shielded from evil and its temptation; and the
road to a rich life lies open to him.

Since he has entered upon the way of life he is delivered from
"the way of evil" (vs. 12). The doctrine of the "two ways,"
which was prominent in later Judaism, concentrates on two
classes of men, the evil and the good. The evil are the slaves of
demonic forces; darkness and perverseness, the crooked and the
devious (vss. 14-15), delight them. The wise reject them, not
only by an act of will but emotionally as well, out of sensibility
and taste.

The wise man is not only delivered from evil men and their
wiles (vss. 12-15) but from the "strange woman" (vss. 16-19,
margin) as well. If the evil men are the slaves of the demonic
forces, this woman is their personification. Chapter 5; 6:20-35;
chapter 7; and 9:13-18 are all devoted to her. She is the antithesis of Wisdom and leads men to death instead of to life. There

is lack of agreement about the interpretation of this figure. Is she a person of flesh and blood, an immoral woman, unfaithful to her husband and her marriage vow (vs. 17), who destroys men by her wiles? And, if so, what is her identity? Is she an Israelite or a foreigner? Or is she simply the personification of evil, since Wisdom is also personified as a woman? Does she represent folly? or apostasy? In subsequent passages the warnings against her involve a man's moral and ethical conduct but also carry a symbolic significance. In the Old Testament, faith and ethics are very closely interrelated, in a manner difficult for the modern secular mind to appreciate. Whatever the nature of the temptation represented by the strange woman, it is deadly in its effect upon those who yield to it: "none . . . come back." But the sage is delivered from its allure, for he knows God and knows how to make right choices. He does not yield to the temptation of either idolatry or adultery.

Finally (vss. 20-22), as a fifth reward, the wise will walk "in the way of good men"; that is, the way of life instead of death. What this means, specifically, is that they "will inhabit the land." In the Old Testament as a whole, Israel's continuance in its land depended upon its obedience to the will of God, which included the obedience of children to their parents (Exod. 20:12); in contrast, the prophets described the Exile as a sign of disobedience. In this poem does "the land" (vss. 21-22) refer to the land of Israel? We cannot be sure. Since national historical facts are never explicitly mentioned in this book, the term may simply refer to any man's life and home. In any case, the wise are those who obey God and live; the wicked are those who disobey him, and they are "cut off." As elsewhere in the Old Testament, so in Proverbs, man's destiny is fulfilled in this life.

Six Expressions of Wisdom and Their Rewards (3:1-12)

A sage exhorts his pupil to follow the way of wisdom and reminds him of the advantages it bestows. First of all (3:1-2) he must remember and keep the instruction of his master, here referred to as "teaching" (*torah*) and "commandments," terms later used exclusively for the Law of Moses. The reward for doing so will be long life and "abundant welfare." This phrase is an attempt to convey something of the fullness of the Hebrew word often translated "peace." It refers to the destiny God intends for one: thus, it is the equivalent of what a Christian today would mean by "salvation." In characteristic Old Testament fashion, however, it refers to a fulfillment in this world, as the phrase "length of days" implies. Long life was a supreme proof of divine favor (Gen. 25:8).

Next (vss. 3-4), let the pupil be constant in "loyalty and faithfulness." These are also words from Israel's religious vocabulary, used of her faith in the Lord and of her faithfulness to him. That reference is not absent here, but the main concern is probably with the teachings of the master and the forms of social conduct these call for. Elsewhere Israelites are urged to bind the words of the Law on their hand and keep them on their heart (Deut. 6:6-9); here the sage's instruction about loyalty and faithfulness receives equivalent status. In human conduct loyalty means mercy and kindness to the helpless (16:6; 20:28; I Kings 20:31; Hosea 4:1). Faithfulness means reliability (see Pss. 15:4; 24:4). The reward? "You will find favor" with "God and man"; that is, you will be an intimate of God and a counselor and leader of men, such as Samuel the prophet became (I Sam. 2:26; see Luke 2:52).

The third admonition (vss. 5-6) is to live a God-centered life: "Trust in the LORD"; "acknowledge him." Any religious outlook as meticulous about the details of human responsibility as was the wisdom movement finds it difficult to remember that man's hope is not in what he can do but in what God will do for him. The danger of deterioration into a religion of works is ever present. There seems little doubt that the wise sometimes did set more store by the way of doing something or the form of saying something than by the basic reason for doing so. Yet, since they confessed that wisdom comes from God and is a part of the mystery of his action manward, they had a built-in antidote to this sort of man-centered idolatry: "do not rely on your own insight." The reward? God will protect and guide you on life's way. In Proverbs there is no fixed formula for correlating the grace of God with man's duty. Nor does one find such a recipe elsewhere in the Bible. In all of Christian history every attempt to define the relation between law and grace has caused division. In Proverbs, and for you and me, these two are constant aspects of the living relationship in which we stand to God. Each enriches the meaning of the other. Both are operative in every decision we make, but in ways that can never be isolated or stated in the abstract.

The fourth admonition (vss. 7-8) is largely a repetition of the third. "Be not wise in your own eyes" can be paraphrased, "Do not take yourself too seriously." A sense of humor is still in season; we are always calling for it—usually in others! It is most badly needed among the "good" people, the "pillars" of society, like the people who produced Proverbs. But what makes a sense of humor possible? It is not to be confused with irresponsibility or flippancy. How can one be serious and relaxed at the same time? Responsible without worrying? The sage replies, "Just remember God is taking care of things." That seems to be a salient meaning for "fear the LORD" here.

In the fifth admonition (vss. 9-10) one is asked to recognize the centrality of God in a more material way, by presenting him with offerings—"substance" and "first fruits." Offerings were joyful acts of thanksgiving for all that God was and did (Deut. 26:1-11). Everything belongs to God (Ps. 50), and he enriches man by making him his steward. These gifts of God are an expression of his goodness. Sacrifice is a joyous act of thanksgiving. In this unit, however, a reward is offered. The belief that the payment of tithes and prescribed offerings was a prerequisite for good yields was characteristic of other traditions in later Judaism (see Mal. 3:8-10). There was a growing tendency to think of offerings as a means to an end rather than as response. The reward? Full barns and bursting wine vats. This sort of deterioration repeats itself also in Christianity.

In his last admonition of the series (vss. 11-12) the sage tells the pupil to be grateful to God for the "discipline" and "reproof" God sends him. He is talking here about the sort of disasters we associate with the case of Job: loss of possessions, security, or health. He would explain these much as Job's friends did: suffering is a token of the love of God; it has a morally purgative function (Job 5:17-19). The issue of justifying the ways of God has here not yet become acute. God disciplines the wise for their own good. The reward for the patient and grateful acceptance of reproof is a deepening awareness of one's filial relation to God, finding God again as the center of one's life.

The Beatitude of Wisdom (3:13-20)

The word "happy" with which this unit begins rests on a Hebrew word which is equal to the Greek word for "blessed" as used in the Beatitudes of the Sermon on the Mount. This is a

beatitude: "Blessed is the man who finds wisdom . . ." In the Old
Testament this literary form with its initial term "happy" or
"blessed" is found mainly in Proverbs (see 8:34; 16:20; 20:7;
28:14; 29:18) and in Psalms which are related to the wisdom
movement (for example, Ps. 1:1). It represents a part of the
movement's contribution to the shaping of the New Testament.
It is a form which in rather subtle fashion combines a pronouncement and a summons. Thus, in this instance the bliss of
the wise man is extolled as a way of persuading men to pursue
the path to wisdom.

Wisdom yields more than gold or silver (vs. 14). All sensate
satisfactions, whatever men "desire" or take delight in (vs. 15),
fall short of the satisfaction wisdom gives. Wisdom is incomparable. The reasons for this are given in the verses that follow.
Those who have wisdom obey the will of God, and this obedience
is rewarded by a long and happy life, something gold and silver
cannot buy. Moreover, those who obey God are also rewarded
with "riches and honor" (vs. 16); and not only these but also
the satisfactions of life implied by "pleasantness, and . . . peace"
are added to the long life of the wise (vss. 17-18). Those who
seek wisdom are like persons in the Gospels who seek first the
Kingdom of God: all other things are granted them in addition
(Matt. 6:33). The supremacy of wisdom as the highest good
does not rest solely, or even mainly, on the fact that long life is
given to the one who possesses it; at least not long life in a
simple, temporal sense. Even fools sometimes have that.

Wisdom was "a tree of life" to those who won her (vs. 18).
In the ancient Near East the tree was a cultic symbol. The tree
stood for the life-giving power of deity (compare Gen. 3:22). It
also stood for those human figures who were thought of as
mediating that life to man, notably the king. Thus the Messiah
to come from the line of King David is "a shoot from the stump
of Jesse" (Isa. 11:1). Therefore to call wisdom "a tree of life"
is not to employ an empty metaphor but a rich symbol. Wisdom,
then, is the life of Deity as available to men. Through it men
participate in the life and purposes of God; and, comparable to
king and Messiah, the wise are themselves mediators of the
divine life. The "long life" wisdom gives is, then, not just life
according to nature but what is later called "eternal life" as
well. This is the real meaning of the beatitude.

Verses 19-20 are really a separate unit, not a part of what

precedes. It anticipates the fuller account of the role of the divine Wisdom in creation in 8:22-31. It is a little hymn to God the Creator. Heaven and earth and the ordered processes of nature, illustrated by clouds and dew, are an expression of the action of God who makes them serve his purposes. The utility and goodness of nature are an expression of God's Wisdom, the same Wisdom he shares with the wise as related in the beatitude above.

Wisdom Gives Serenity of Life (3:21-24)

In some ways this unit repeats what is found in 3:1-4. But the exhortation to seek wisdom is motivated here not so much by the reputation and honor it brings to its possessor as by the sense of security and absence of fear it brings. Calmness, poise, self-control, and rationality were all qualities cultivated by devotees of the wisdom movement. The fact that the movement flourished in court circles helps account for the rejection of impetuosity and emotionalism. In some respects this characteristic deportment was simply a matter of habitual and controlled response or conscious self-discipline. But there is more to it than that; one does not argue one's self into a sense of security or into the relaxation of calm sleep. For the sages, in the last analysis, serenity rested on faith in God, a faith that made compulsiveness about security or courage unnecessary.

What to Avoid and Why (3:25-35)

This section presents a series of six prohibitions which, with the exception of the first (vs. 25), deal with the ethics of social relations. A man must support a worthy cause or person according to his ability and must not put off doing it; the wise are not to live entirely in a world apart, however much they may have sought each other's company. Their teachings were to be exemplified in their social behavior. A series of four antithetical couplets follows to make clear the reasons for the prohibitions.

A Father's Legacy to His Son (4:1-9)

Wisdom, the "fear of God" that enables one to think straight and choose wisely, is the greatest treasure. It is also the most precious bequest a father can give to his son. In Israel it is acknowledged that a father is a son's first teacher, just as he is his first priest. The professional sages are only an extension of a parental function, not a substitute for it. Here we have a picture of a father playing the role of a teacher of wisdom. "I give you good precepts," he says. The term for "precepts" is a singular noun meaning "that which is received"; thus in this case it means a bequest of wisdom from father to son. Wisdom is something that can be handed on; there is a "tradition" of wisdom which is the means by which wisdom comes alive in each succeeding generation. Ancient Israel assumed that "religion can be taught"; the wisdom movement, especially, worked with this assumption. Like all groups that place high value upon tradition, it was both conservative and tenacious as a cultural force.

The father addressing his sons speaks of his own youth. He was very precious to his mother (vs. 3). In Proverbs the mother shares the educational task with the father and is equally deserving of respect. Solomon's mother pinned great hopes on him; he was her "only one" (see I Kings 1:11-21), and Solomon credits his choice of wisdom to his father David (I Kings 3:3-14). These things may be in the mind of this poet: he makes every father a Solomon in his role as sage and teacher to his sons.

It is not enough, however, to remember what one has been taught (vs. 5a), important as that is. One must "get wisdom." This expression carries with it the notion of acquisition by purchase; a man must "buy" it, in the only way it can be "bought," by concentrating on it—"whatever you *get, get* insight"! The merchant who found the pearl of great price (Matt. 13:45-46) is a perfect illustration of this father's attitude and probably owes something to this passage. The "beginning of wisdom," the very heart of it (see 1:7), is the desire for it. One who has that is already wise. To love God is to serve him.

To underscore the incomparability of wisdom once more, this father compares her to a bride (vss. 8-9; compare 7:4). For a good wife no bride price is too high (see 18:22; 19:14; 31:10-31). One is to be faithful to wisdom as to a good wife (vs. 6). Those who love, protect, and embrace her will receive the crown of honor she bestows (vs. 9; Song of Solomon 3:11).

The Two Ways (4:10-19)

The theme of the two ways, here compared to light and darkness (vss. 18-19), is used once again to exalt the quest for

knowledge of God and his works and to contrast it with the life
of those who do not think that knowledge is important. In
Proverbs we generally find two contrasting pairs: "wise-fools"
and "righteous-wicked." Here the wise (vs. 11) are set over
against the "wicked" (vs. 14). This style occurs hardly at all
in chapters 10-31.

The sage repeats the now familiar admonitions in exhorting
his pupil: Heed my words and you will have a long life (vs.
10); guided by the knowledge you have received from me you
will avoid the pitfalls of life and "not stumble" (vs. 12). But his
outburst of acclaim lacks the inspiration and the profundity
of the one immediately preceding it. It seems almost perfunctory
by comparison, and lacking in originality. The contrast is most
easily illustrated by the fact that wisdom here is never personified;
it is simply the words and the way taught by the sage. More is
made of holding onto it and guarding it (vs. 13) than of the
protection and honor it gives to those who prize it (4:6). What
seems to be missing here that was so fully present in the earlier
unit is the awareness that one who really loves wisdom and the
God who is its source is preoccupied with it and not with evil.
Hence the lengthy warning against "the path of the wicked" and
its abominations.

Perhaps the most penetrating observation comes with the
recognition of the progressive character of wisdom and wickedness respectively. A thing grows by what it feeds on, and the
wicked feed on wickedness and quench the thirst of life with "the
wine of violence" (vs. 17). One is reminded, in contrast, of the
word of Jesus, "My food is to do the will of him who sent me"
(John 4:34). The career of the wise also involves development;
they grow in clarity of understanding, just as approaching day
brightens "the light of dawn" (vs. 18).

On Target (4:20-27)

The stringent control and singleness of purpose inculcated in
this section remind one of the mechanically controlled space
instruments one reads about today. Everything depends on
whether they are "on target"; and one marvels at the accuracy
of the electronic devices that keep them there. The writers of
Proverbs believed that wisdom, well taught and faithfully used,
can accomplish a comparable result. It keeps a man moving
toward the target called "life."

Except for verses 23 and 26 this unit consists of parallelistic couplets in which the second line is a synonym of the first. The employment of this form of parallelism, which emphasizes an idea by reiterating it rather than by citing its opposite, probably occurs here because it is an artistic device to accentuate the author's concern with a single focus. Nothing extraneous must interfere with the course that lies straight ahead. Read the text aloud to get the feel of the impact that is intended. The spell woven by the reiteration of ideas and the massing of synonymous terms is enhanced by the fact that the pupil is never given a chance to let his attention wander from himself. The doubled imperatives are all directed at him, and there are no references to any other person, evil or good, nor to anything else outside the person addressed. Here the stern old sage, with his eye on his pupil, and his finger pointed straight at him, the imperatives rolling out, says, "You, I mean you!" in about the most emphatic way in which it can be said.

This calculated effort to create a mood and make an impact gives us a clue to how the writer feels about wisdom. His words are not just a bit of practical advice to guide a man and bring him success; they must become a life principle, resident within the heart (vs. 21). The biblical word "heart" comes close to our idea of "mind"; it can be paraphrased as "conscious and rational intention." This intention or attitude contains "the springs of life" which determine all our words and deeds. A man is what he intends.

The lively concern to have his pupil remain "on target," to which this poet has devoted all of his great artistic skill, finally comes to open expression in verse 25: "eyes . . . directly forward . . . , gaze . . . straight." It happens again in verse 27: "Do not swerve to the right or to the left." The intense singleness of purpose inculcated by this section reappears frequently in the teachings of Jesus (for example, Matt. 5:20-48; 18:8-9).

Wisdom and the Strange Woman (5:1-23)

Wisdom is the knowledge and experience about life and living taught and explained by the sages; it is a pupil's capacity for mature and right understanding and judgment, a capacity which results when he fully comprehends and chooses as his own what he is taught; and, finally, wisdom is the action and intention of God at work in the life of a man who has heard the teachings,

really understood them, and chosen them as his own. In this
last sense it is very similar to what Christians understand by the
illumination of the Holy Spirit.

In verse 1, as frequently in the preceding units (1:8; 2:1; 3:1;
4:1, 10, 20), "wisdom" is used in the first of the three senses
cited above. This is rather natural since, in its form, it is a
teacher's admonition to his pupil. The teacher knows as well as
any teacher today that his words by themselves will not be
enough, that a man must find wisdom (3:13) and accept his
words (4:10) for himself. He also knows that only if a man
recognizes the presence of the hand of God in all this, ex-
periencing "the fear of the LORD" (1:7), will he really be wise.
But, like a preacher or teacher today, he concentrates on his
own part. This is doubly true since, as a good sage, he believes
that the divine Wisdom and its illumination and power are
granted only to those who have really learned and deliberately
chosen as a result of this. He knows that his words alone do not
shield a man from evil; only the Wisdom of God, operative in
a man who responds to it, can do that. But a man cannot choose
or respond unless he has been taught; belief does depend on
hearing (see Rom. 10:14-17).

This chapter consists of three sections: verses 1-6, 7-14, and
15-23. They are closely related and all deal with the "loose
woman" first encountered in 2:16-19. The adjective "loose"
conveys the notion of adultery or sexual licentiousness, but the
term means "strange" (2:16, see margin). It is applied to one
who does not belong, an outsider. It is applied to those outside
a family (Ps. 109:11), to those outside the nation (Hosea 7:9;
8:7, "aliens"), and, in worship, to unauthorized rites (Exod.
30:9; Num. 3:4, "unholy"). Thus the "strange woman" (or
"loose woman") is someone who does not belong. She could be
taken literally as a harlot who does not belong in a family, as an
"alien" who does not belong in Israel, or as a personified symbol
of religious belief or practice that is unauthorized. It is likely
that all the sections on this "loose woman" combine the first and
third of these possibilities. In them the sages do issue a reminder
to their pupils of the folly of unchastity and promiscuity and of
the evil results that flow from them. But this may be only
incidental to the attack these passages make upon Dame Folly,
the personified embodiment of foolishness, of all that is the
opposite of wisdom and good sense. Wisdom is a true lady

(1:20-33; 8:1-21, 22-36; 9:1-12), the chosen of God. She proclaims the truth, points men to the true and the good, and gives them the gift of life. But Folly, her rival for the attention of men (2:16-19; 5:1-23; 7:1-27; 9:13-18), is a slut, the siren of Death and the Underworld. She seduces men with cunning temptations but ends by destroying them, body and soul. Sexual immorality is only one part of the activity of this Dame Folly, though a conspicuous one. What we have in Proverbs 1-9, with respect to these two characters, is a very high example of literary imagination and artistic skill.

For the wisdom movement, of course, foolishness and wickedness constituted apostasy. If wisdom was the means and vehicle for the work of the true and living God, folly and wickedness served the power or powers that opposed him. The prophets had described heresy and apostasy as adultery: Israel played the harlot by going after other gods (Jer. 2:1-37; Ezek. 16, 23; Hosea 1-3). The author of Proverbs 1-9 was therefore dealing in a familiar pattern of metaphors when he portrayed Wisdom as a chaste and faithful bride and Folly as an adulterous and apostate harlot. Sages, like the prophets, condemned all forms of immorality, though in Proverbs references to sexual sins are relatively infrequent (22:14; 23:26-28; 29:3; 30:20; 31:3). But both viewed it as an expression of a more deep-seated infidelity—lack of commitment to God. Ethical and social conduct they treated as the by-product of one's whole attitude to life, that is, of one's faith in God, or lack of it. Does the Church today follow their example? Or is it too eager to make a case for ethical conduct on purely practical and rational grounds? In the Bible, love of God and love of man go together; the former supports the latter and dies without it.

In the first section of this homily (5:1-6) the author exposes the "woman" as a fraud. Her seductive speech, "smoother than oil" (vs. 3), might deceive a pupil if he were not forewarned; therefore the teacher sketches the path of death (vs. 5) traveled by those who are taken in by her.

But why is she so seductive? What is the appeal of idolatry? What really makes a harlot attractive? The answer to the questions is basically the same: they seem to offer men *the luxury of irresponsibility and self-centeredness*. The service of the living God demands obedience to a reality outside one's self. Israel lived in covenant with God who had saved her; but his grace called for the response of thanksgiving and loyalty. "Thy will be done" stands for the God-centeredness of biblical faith. One must become a servant, "captive to the Word of God" as Luther put it. This goes against the grain in a man who wants to be his own master. He prefers an idol to the living God. For an idol, whatever its form, is finally always a projection of one's self and of one's own desires. The worship of idols is self-worship, not self-surrender but self-indulgence. This is just as true when it takes the form of ascetic self-discipline as when it is expressed in hedonistic self-indulgence. The idolator is irresponsible because he is self-centered. He tries to take the place of God, and to decide what he is and what he wants. This is the attraction of Dame Folly as the embodiment of idolatry or apostasy.

But if Folly be viewed primarily as a harlot the situation is the same. The basic allure of adultery and promiscuity is that it seems to offer something for nothing; it appeals to irresponsibility. The "woman," as a harlot, calls for no commitment or covenant obligation, no reciprocity as in marriage. The adulterer, like the idolator, wants to be his own master; he will not bear a yoke of responsibility or commit himself to live for another. The wise men and prophets did a profound thing when they chose harlotry as the metaphor for idolatry; both express unfaithfulness because both are motivated by self-centeredness and irresponsibility. But just because of this both are self-destructive, for "whoever would save his life will lose it" (Matt. 16:25).

In verses 7-14 the self-destruction of the fornicator is sketched in strokes familiar to all: his folly costs him his "honor" and reputation; he gives his substance to an "alien" on whose loyalty he has no claim; and he comes to the end of his days lonely and full of remorse (vss. 9-11). Then, in his remorse, he thinks of what might have been: If he had only been a willing pupil, who had not "hated discipline," and who had listened to his teachers (vss. 12-13), he would have been a sage. He had not simply broken his marriage vows or the moral conventions of society; as an apostate sage he had also flouted his covenant with God, so that he was a fool before God as well as before men.

Finally (vss. 15-23), the author issues a call to faithfulness. On the face of it this is an appeal for faithfulness in marriage; it is well to begin to study it by taking it as such. It is a beautifully delicate and imaginative paragraph. The author's moralistic warning tone has been displaced by one that is all romanticism and enthusiasm. "Drink water from your own cistern" (vs. 15). "Let your fountain be blessed" (vs. 18). Cistern, well, spring, fountain: these are all metaphors for wife (Ps. 68:26; Song of Solomon 4:12, 15). But, it is well to note, they are also metaphors for God. These verses eulogize the sensuous enjoyment of marriage in a wholesome and uninhibited manner, much as does the Song of Solomon. They are so winsome because they are so natural and free from stuttering self-consciousness.

At verse 20 the romantic spell is over; the stern moral teacher comes back. Why would you want to fall for "a loose woman"? After the eulogy about married love just preceding there can only be one answer: there is nothing to be gained by it. So he warns again of the destruction that would surely be produced. The logic is perfect; moreover, the emotional weight remains on the side of virtue, for the harlot is not described.

As it stands, the third section is a powerful plea for marital fidelity. But, set as it is in the context of the wisdom movement, with its concern to know the will of God and thus to participate in his action, it can also be read as a plea for fidelity to God and the search for his wisdom. And then what it warns against is not adultery but idolatry.

Four Brief Discourses (6:1-19)

The subject of wisdom as the only sure protection against the evil woman is briefly laid aside. Four sections, verses 1-5, 6-11, 12-15, and 16-19, briefer and more concrete in their references than most of the discourses in chapters 1-9, are introduced. Brief as they are, however, they are in the style of little essays in contrast to the aphoristic style that begins at chapter 10.

Prudence and Suretyship (6:1-5)

The first of these little essays issues a warning about serving as a surety or guarantor for another man. It is not clear what form of particular responsibility is referred to. Suretyship for debt was probably the most common form of pledge-giving, but it might also be a personal bond (Gen. 43:9). The pledge was made by the clasping of hands and the taking of an oath while so doing. Once having committed himself in this way a man was caught, for a word sealed by an oath could not be broken (Num. 30:2). Notices often appear in the public press to the effect that after a given date a named person will "no longer be responsible for debts" contracted by another named person whose surety he has been up to that point. Such legal recourse for terminating a pledge to serve as surety does not seem to have existed in Israel. The only way to terminate the agreement would be by the action of the beneficiary on whose behalf it was made.

In Israel, of course, there was a standing obligation that one had toward one's own family in matters of this sort. As illustrated by the story of Ruth, the "next of kin" had a moral obligation to take responsibility for the debts of his relative, if he was able to do so (Ruth 4:1-6). In Proverbs we are not dealing with pledges to relatives but to others, whether "neighbor" or "stranger" (vs. 1). The sages, as a matter of general principle, felt it was unwise to undertake pledges for such people (11:15; 17:18; 22:26). Among us, too, there is a difference of opinion about the advisability of making "private loans" as an act of neighborliness and secured only by friendship and trust. Some hold it is uncharitable not to do so; others feel that in a case such as this prudence should outweigh sentiment. That was the view of the writers of Proverbs. Considering the absence of any legal means of redress one can understand the counsel they gave.

This little essay is concerned entirely with ways and means of canceling this sort of pledge. Until this occurs one is pictured as "snared in the utterance" of his lips (vs. 2); that is, he is the victim of a pledge made thoughtlessly or in a moment of well-meaning emotional excitement. The victim must "save" himself (vss. 3, 5), or give himself no rest (vs. 4) until he gets out of his trap. He is caught in his neighbor's power (vs. 3); a sword hangs constantly over his head. But what can he do? He has no legal recourse of his own. Even in his desire to terminate the arrangement he is at the mercy of his "neighbor," who has everything to gain by refusing to remit the oath. But there is no other way: he must hasten and "importune" this man. That is, he must make such a nuisance of himself with his client, by his endless and harassing efforts to get a release, that the latter will finally decide that he would rather cancel the agreement than continue to enjoy its advantages under such circumstances. One is, of course, reminded of the parable of Jesus about the importunate widow (Luke 18:1-8).

On Indolence and Poverty (6:6-11)

The second section (vss. 6-11) deals with industry, which

ranks with prudence as one of the great virtues encouraged by Proverbs. The book holds that, normally at least, human misfortune is avoidable. Poverty is one such misfortune, and it is the result of sloth (10:4; 12:11; 20:13; 23:21; 24:33-34; 28:19). The ant is wise (see also 30:25) in respect to industry, and those seeking wisdom can learn from her: she has foresight. At harvest time she stores up food for all the winter months to come (vs. 8); what is more, she does this as a matter of personal choice, not at the command of any imposed authority. The teacher endows the insect with all the individualism, reason, and will power of a true sage! Having told him about the ant, the sage taunts the sluggard with his dallying. The fort against poverty remains unmanned, and once poverty is admitted, it cannot be driven out (vss. 10-11).

On Subversion (6:12-15)

Proverbs finds cunning and maliciousness contemptible (see 16:27-30). Talebearing, misrepresentation to create conflict, false charges to generate discord: these are works of the wicked which the wise must avoid. In the Babylonian Code of Hammurabi the punishment for a charge falsely made was inflicted upon the one who brought the charge (see also Exod. 23:1). This writer of Proverbs would have approved of that kind of punishment.

Seven Sins (6:16-19)

This list of sins is remarkably similar to the evils attributed to the subversive. The number "seven" carries the notion of completeness (24:16; 26:16, 25). What may be intended is: "Here is the whole list of qualities that make up a sneak and a troublemaker" (keeping in mind the apparent connection with the preceding passage). The use of "six things . . . seven" in the parallelism is a common device in the use of numbers (see 30:18, 21, 29; Amos 1:3, 6, 9, 11, 13; 2:1, 4). "Seven" survived as a "perfect number" in Christian tradition. Thus "The Seven Deadly Sins" could be paraphrased as "The sins that sum up all sin."

On the Peril of Adultery (6:20-35)

Following the interlude of the four little essays we seem, at first glance, to resume the portrayal of the contest between Lady Wisdom and Dame Folly for the hearts of men which was featured in chapter 5. There are no doubt affinities between the two sections, for chapter 5 is concerned with sexual transgression as well as with apostasy (see the comment). But in this section the concern with apostasy and the treatment of the "woman" as the personified antithesis of Wisdom seem to be absent. The term "loose woman" (or "strange woman") does not appear here. It is the "evil woman" (vs. 24), or, in the Septuagint version, "the wife of one's neighbor." From verse 27 to the end of the chapter the preoccupation is directly and unambiguously with one particular form of sexual sin, namely, adultery. From this it seems legitimate to conclude, as the translators seem to have done in attempting to reconstruct the garbled text of verse 26, that this whole section is about this one form of infidelity.

Adultery involves the breaking of a marriage contract. Hence, in ancient Israel, it was more severely punished than any other form of promiscuity; both parties involved were to be put to death, by stoning (Deut. 22:22; Ezek. 18:10-13). Thus it was treated as severely as murder. A wife was a man's possession, paid for with a bride price. Adultery involved moral depravity; it was also a severe offense against the economic and social order. This may help to explain why it was dealt with much more severely than fornication. It may be noted, for example, that in the Ten Commandments the prohibition is, literally speaking, against adultery only. Harlots were under certain social stigmas and religious disabilities (Lev. 21:7); in some respects they may even have been despised, though the tenor of narratives such as found in Genesis 38 and Joshua 2 does not reveal it. Surely for a woman to become a prostitute or harlot was degrading (Lev. 19:29), but harlots were not put to death, unless they were adulteresses as well. And, as in Arab lands today, for a man to visit a harlot constituted no legal offense. All of this is presupposed in the section on adultery, where the pupil is warned about the dreadful revenge that will be taken by the outraged husband (vss. 33-35).

Wisdom, here presented as a "father's commandment" (vs. 20; see also 4:1) and a "mother's teaching," will show a man the folly of adultery and serve to protect him from it. In greater detail than in 3:1-3 we have in verses 20-23 a medley of metaphors usually associated with the Mosaic Law, but now used to extol this instruction: verses 21-22 paraphrase Deuteronomy 6:6-7; and verse 23 is reminiscent of Psalm 119:105. The parental teachings "will lead," they will guard, and they "will talk with you." That is, they will become a part of one's very personality through having been repeated so often and thought about in so many situations. Repetition and memory figured very prominently in the educational method of the sages. They have been too greatly discounted, perhaps, by modern educational theorists. Hymns and prayers memorized in childhood often become the means for development into religious maturity.

The deadly risk involved in adultery is set forth in the illustrations of the "fire" and "coals" (vss. 27-28). Anyone who seduces his "neighbor's wife" (vs. 29), or yields to her advances, will be burned. A thief when caught must make multiple restitution ("sevenfold" in verse 31 must not be taken literally, but in the sense of "full" or "complete"). But the adulterer will suffer an infinitely greater penalty. He has not only taken a man's most valuable possession in an economic sense; by taking her he invaded her husband's life, for the family is a psychic unity, a single life. Adultery destroys it. In Israelite psychology the adulterer is literally a murderer and is worthy of a murderer's fate. One who has suffered loss by theft may be willing to settle for a restitution of property. But the offended husband cannot be appeased even by multiple compensation (vs. 35); he will exact the death penalty the law prescribes.

The Shield of Wisdom (7:1-27)

Chapter 7 ponders another discourse on the contest between wisdom and "the loose woman" for the possession of the hearts of men. In its basic concerns it corresponds to chapter 5. It condemns vice and adultery and uses them as illustrations of unfaithfulness to wisdom. That is, the profligate and the apostate are dealt with simultaneously (see the comment on ch. 5). What is new in this discourse is the utilization of dramatic forms to depict the allure of Folly and the progressive destruction of those who heed her call. In a series of realistic tableaux (vss. 6-9, 10-20, 21-23) it tells how a naïve and untutored lad is lured into evil and led to his death. What is assumed throughout—and this is the real point of the discourse—is that if he had been taught the way of wisdom, he could have saved himself. Wisdom, a real understanding of God and his way in the world, is man's only shield in the battle of life.

The Prologue (7:1-5)

The introduction of the discourse begins with the familiar admonition to "keep" and "treasure up" the "words," "commandments," or "teachings" that convey the true and the good. As we look back over the growing list of such admonitions (2:1-4; 3:1, 21-22; 4:1-2, 20-21; 5:1; 6:20-21) we are impressed by accumulations of synonyms. Wisdom is designated as words, commandments, understanding, insight, teaching, discretion, instruction, precepts, and sayings. All are fully interchangeable and all point to knowledge of God. Man's struggle to possess this wisdom is likewise encouraged by means of an ever-growing vocabulary. He must receive, treasure up, be attentive to, incline his heart to, cry out for, seek, remember, keep, hear, incline his ear to, bind on his heart, tie about his neck, and now (7:3) bind on his fingers, and write on the "tablet" of his mind ("heart") this instruction. In this list, also, any word or term in the list is fully exchangeable with all of the others. The multiplication of synonyms simply shows how clearly the subject was understood and how important it was considered to be. The goal of both the seeking and the keeping is wisdom—to be wise, to know the way of God so that one may know how to live.

Such singleness of purpose is summed up in verse 4 of this Prologue: "Say to wisdom, 'You are my sister.' " In the wisdom literature of Egypt, "sister" is a term for bride. This is also the case in the Song of Solomon (for example, 4:9). What is said here is: "Marry wisdom, accept her as your bride." In the parallel line that follows, the pupil is told to call her his "intimate friend." The real meaning of the Hebrew word so translated is "kinsman" (Ruth 2:1). A kinsman was a close male relative on whose protection one could lay claim. The parallel lines of verse 4 are synonymous in meaning, but the synonym is contained in the equating of wisdom with insight, not of "sister" with "intimate friend." The point of the verse is the protection found in wisdom: just as the kinsman is the best protection against the creditor (see 6:1-5) and a good marriage (see 5:15-20) against a prostitute, so wisdom is the shield to preserve "from the loose woman" (vs. 5; see comment on 5:1-23). She is the embodiment of evil and foolishness, the denial of God and his moral rule.

The Seduction (7:6-23)

The first scene (vss. 6-9) in the dramatic account of the

destruction of the simple youth by the evil woman takes us to a
room in the house of the sage. (In the Septuagint the scene takes
place in the woman's house; she is looking out of her window to
spy potential victims.) As is common in oriental cities even
today, the sage has access to a trellised window, probably on the
second floor, facing on a street or overlooking a city square
(Judges 5:28). Here, unnoticed, he can sit in reflective quiet
and take note of the ever-changing scene below. The sages made
a specialty of observing the human parade as a source for their
understanding of man's situation. It is the time of evening twi-
light (vs. 9); simple youths crowd the thoroughfare. The simple
are vulnerable to all sorts of dangers because they can neither
discriminate between appeals made to them nor realize the
further implications of a course of action.

A notorious woman's house is located in the sage's field of
vision. He knows about it; and he notices that "a young man
without sense," from the crowd of simple ones, leaves the square
and takes the road that leads to her house. We may surmise that
his action is premeditated. He may have heard about this place and
wants to satisfy his curiosity. If he is expressing any real initiative, it will soon be taken out of his hands.

This becomes clear in the second scene (vss. 10-20), which
gives us a close-up of the "loose woman" in her seductive appeal
to the naïve youth. The woman, who is presented as having a
husband (vs. 19), comes out of her house dressed as a harlot
(see Gen. 38:14-15), to make her intentions unmistakably clear,
and, perhaps, to allay fear; for a professional harlot, who was
not any man's wife, represented no great risk.

The action halts for a moment (vss. 11-12) while we are
given a brief biographical note on her. She is shameless and
restless in her seductive desire; "her feet do not stay at home"
(vs. 11). Adultery has become a habit and a disease for this
wife. The sketch corresponds to the one the prophet Jeremiah
gives us about Israel as the unfaithful bride (Jer. 2:23-25, 33-37;
3:2).

The action resumes. The woman reduces to zero what little
power of reason the youth possesses. She says she has a rich
meal waiting since she has just paid her "vows" which entailed
the offering of sacrifices. The vow of the Nazirite (Num. 6:1-21)
and other individual vows were terminated by the offering of an
animal sacrifice. This entailed eating some of the sacrificial meat
at home within a prescribed period of time (Lev. 7:16-18). The

offering of a sacrifice was always the occasion for a feast. Passover and the other communal festivals included sacrificial meals for all celebrants. In the case of individual occasions the guests were often numerous.

In this scene the feast is used only as an excuse to introduce the woman's real purpose. Many interpreters of these discourses on "the strange woman" think she represents the Canaanite goddess of fertility. They hold that the sages had a specific cult in mind when they presented the woman as the embodiment of apostasy in contrast to the faithfulness to the God of Israel represented by wisdom. They support their view that a fertility cult was involved in the form of apostasy combatted by the sages by pointing out that the invitation to "love" in verses 16-18 has affinities with the descriptions of the "sacred marriage" which was a feature of the fertility cult rites. On the other hand, although the "woman" is a symbol of apostasy as well as the example of immorality (see the comment on 5:1-21), there is not enough clear evidence to show that a particular form of apostasy is intended. The exotic language and metaphors used in this scene are obviously not original with the author, as a casual reading of the Song of Solomon will make clear. He is using selected portions of a stock of forms and expressions that seems quite fixed, and relatively conventional. That much of this stock of materials originated in non-Israelite religious liturgies that contained the sexual motifs of a fertility cult seems most probable. But it does not necessarily follow that we have to do here with an example of that actual alien cult as such. This, it seems, is reinforced by the fact that at verse 19 the speech turns to a feature that would not have anything to do with such a cult liturgy: "my husband is not at home." These words take us back to a concrete flesh-and-blood scene. The woman is an adulteress: she plays the harlot during her husband's absence; and yet, she is more than just an adulterous wife: she is the "strange woman" in a life-and-death struggle with wisdom, her "negative equal," as it were. And the youth is not just one victim of seduction. He is that, but he is also every man faced with the choice between life and death.

The third scene (vss. 21-23) emphasizes the finality that is involved in yielding to the woman's seduction. The young man yields and follows "as an ox goes to the slaughter" (vs. 22); "it will cost him his life" (vs. 23). Taken descriptively, as part of a real story, this means that the husband will return and kill the boy—and the woman, his wife. Or he will have the legally appointed officers do so. This is one way in which it may cost him his life; but it is not the only way, or the most profound. We are not here dealing only in physical life. Besides, the woman in these discourses is a more perennial aspect of existence than a wayward wife in Israel ever was, even if she had deluded her husband and died a natural death. This woman invites men to death, but never dies!

The Epilogue (7:24-27)

In his peroration the sage returns to his introduction: only the teachings of wisdom can protect you. Do not "stray into her paths" (vs. 25). The woman's "slain are a mighty host." The woman's "house is the way to Sheol." She is the equal but opposite of wisdom, whose "house" (9:1) is the portal to life. The practical wisdom of Egypt and Babylon, as well as of Israel, warned against adultery and promiscuity on prudential grounds similar to those current among us. In these discourses on the "loose woman" the sage who probably edited Proverbs has given these old themes about chastity and faithfulness a new motivation; he has made them parables of faithfulness to God as revealed in the wisdom taught by the sages. And their opposites, promiscuity and infidelity, consequently become parables of apostasy to alien cults or of the foolishness of the fool who says in his heart that there is no God (Ps. 14:1).

The Invitation of Wisdom (8:1-21)

The sages frequently personify wisdom. That is, they consider wisdom a living entity, endowed with life and motion. Wisdom is more than information and principles that men gather and develop. Wisdom is referred to as a person, as "she" rather than "it"; and the word becomes "Wisdom," a proper noun. Treated in this way, the sages frequently eulogize Wisdom as the greatest security man has and as the resource for all his understanding (for example, Job 28). In this role she is thought of as either reluctant to share herself wholly with man or as fully available to him. But there is an even greater honor the sages pay this living Wisdom than to offer eulogies on her behalf; and that is to let her speak for herself. An example of this is found in Proverbs 1:20-33. Chapter 8 presents two more (vss. 4-21, 22-36).

As in 1:20-33, Wisdom appears here as a preacher. To deliver her message she visits the same public places frequented by her deadly adversary, the "loose woman" (7:11-12). In 1:20-33 she came as a prophetic preacher of repentance. She issued judgments against scorners and warned of their impending destruction. Here she comes as an evangelist. She is the preacher of good tidings. She proclaims that she has the gifts that will bring men to their true fulfillment, and that she offers these gifts freely to all.

There is no hint that the invitation Wisdom offers is for Jews only. There is no reference to a special revelation, a historical event such as the Exodus of Israel, or the Covenant at Sinai based on this, on the basis of which this proclamation is made. One is given the very definite impression that the writers of Proverbs assumed that this good news of Wisdom was as accessible to an Egyptian as to an Israelite. Only later did the wisdom movement of Israel return to the particularism implicit in historical revelation and election which are central themes of biblical faith.

The writers of Proverbs were familiar with much of the religious vocabulary of Judaism, particularly as related to the Law. The ethos of the faith of Israel no doubt influenced them in many ways, both personally and ethically. There is no evidence that they were consciously in rebellion against the particularity of historical revelation; nevertheless, it cannot be gainsaid that they ignore this central theme of biblical faith and, in postulating the revelatory function of Wisdom, provide what amounts to an alternative for it. Proverbs lacks a doctrine of sin which separates the order of creation from the order of redemption. In Wisdom, God makes himself known and available to all men without reference to such particular historical events as Exodus or Jesus Christ or to the communities that rest on these.

This chapter—and indeed the whole of the first nine chapters of Proverbs—while ignoring the particularity of Israel's faith, does stress its theocentricity; that is, man is what he is, in the last analysis, by the fact that God acts in his behalf. Thus, Wisdom is the action of God that enables men to know what is true and good.

Wisdom the evangelist comes into the midst of the human

scene (vss. 1-3) to make her announcement; on the heights, beside the way, in the paths, she raises her voice and calls. The piling up of synonyms stresses the urgency of the matter: Wisdom is ready to go anywhere, even "to the highways and hedges" (Luke 14:23). Such is the love and concern of God for man, for Wisdom here is the action of God.

Wisdom speaks to all (vss. 4-5). The "simple" and "foolish" can learn if they will; and those who seek will "find" (vs. 17; see Matt. 7:7). Man must respond and co-operate with God; the Pauline concept that even the response and co-operation are acts of God (Phil. 2:13) is lacking here, or at least it is not made explicit.

In Wisdom, God speaks what is true and right (vss. 6-9). "God is light and in him is no darkness at all" (I John 1:5) is a New Testament equivalent of what is being said here: no man, however well-intentioned, can speak unambiguously; there is error in all his truth, and self-centeredness in all his goodness. The modern emphasis upon the conditionedness and relativity of all things created and human draws attention to this. Even the sages could not wholly phrase the truth and goodness Wisdom proclaimed.

The self-disclosure of God in Wisdom, his personal seeking of man through what we could call the Holy Spirit, is man's greatest treasure (vss. 10-13). Treasures of silver and gold decay; the incomparability of the action of God in search of man consists in the fact that it never ends. Therefore, "lay up for yourselves treasures in heaven" (Matt. 6:19-21), says the divine Wisdom.

The royal authority and the judicial insight of kings and rulers, says Wisdom, is mediated to them by her (vss. 14-17). In the ancient Near East, kingship was thought to have been established by the gods in the initial cosmological ordering of existence. The king represents and embodies the authority of deity. He has access to divine wisdom by virtue of his post. He rules by "divine right." Hammurabi declared that he was the "sun of Babylon," that is, the vicegerent of the god Marduk, and that as such he had "plumbed the depth of wisdom." Many aspects of these ideas about the role and nature of the king were also present in Israel. The king was the Messiah, the divinely anointed; he was the adopted son of God (see Ps. 2:7); and, conspicuously in the case of Solomon, he had access to divine counsel and judicial skill. It is very difficult for most moderns to sense the distinctiveness of an office apart from the personality of its occupant. How can one say that the divine Wisdom acts by means of a wicked or foolish king? or, turning it around, that such a king has access to the divine Wisdom? It is one thing to say it about Solomon; but how can it be said about the wicked Manasseh? Yet the conviction that the Wisdom of God, as political power, is mediated through all sorts of rulers is persistent in Scripture. The Assyrian is the "rod" of God's anger, declares Isaiah (Isa. 10:5); and Paul (Rom. 13:1-5) advocates obedience to the political authorities because of their status as rulers, not because of their personal character.

Wisdom ends with the promise (vss. 18-21) that those who "love" her (vs. 21) will have as a bonus all they have forsaken in order to respond to her message (Matt. 6:33). Honor and wealth come to those who serve God. This is a central theme not only of Proverbs but of most of the Old Testament. It is a theme subjected to severe re-examination in the Book of Job; but there it is not so much abolished as redefined. This also holds for the New Testament. It must be noticed finally in this proclamation of Wisdom that what she really offers is herself. To be sure, the lore and intelligence the sages display come from her; so do good character and keen insight in a man. The action of God in Wisdom can and must be described by these. But what really makes a man rich is the very fact of the action of God on his behalf, and the availability of it. This is the divine Wisdom; in her, God offers himself to man.

The First-Born of All Creation (8:22-36)

In the discourse in 8:4-21 Wisdom presented herself to men as their greatest good, the inexhaustible source of their life. Now, in this discourse she deals specifically with the reasons for this. Before God created anything else he created Wisdom; she is "the first-born of all creation" (see Col. 1:15). Before fountains and springs, and older than the eternal hills, is Wisdom. Before God began to do anything else he "brought forth" Wisdom. The discourse makes this point for two reasons: (1) To claim for Wisdom the incomparable excellence of primacy, and (2) to show that she has a hand in all that is.

In Israel the first-born was believed to be endowed with an advantage (Gen. 49:3). This expressed itself practically in the share of his inheritance; in the authority he exercised over the family, under his father; and perhaps most significantly in the fact that, in the rites of the dedication and redemption of the first-born, he represented the family in its relation to God. This well-understood role of the first-born in Israelite society is here used to exalt the status of Wisdom in relation to the rest of God's creation. Like Jesus Christ, Wisdom is "the first-born"; she is the Alpha (see Rev. 22:13).

In Christian history the heretical movement called Arianism held that Jesus Christ was a created being, that he was not co-eternal with the Father but that "there was a time when he was not." Arians appealed to this section of Proverbs and to the way it is applied to Christ in Colossians 1:15 and elsewhere in the New Testament. If we were to think of Wisdom here as a real and distinct person, called into existence at a given moment of time, no matter how long ago, their contention would, of course, be unanswerable. But here, as in all of these discourses, Wisdom is a personified attribute of God rather than an independent person created by him. She is the divine intelligence personified, just as elsewhere the "arm of the LORD" (Isa. 51:9) personifies his power. Wisdom here is not an eternal being; but she is an eternal attribute of the creative action of God. The poet has difficulty in finding the right words to say what he wants to say; namely, that God has always possessed this attribute and never acts without it.

The word "created" here rests on a Hebrew term meaning "acquired." God acquired Wisdom "at the beginning" (vs. 22), "at the first" (vs. 23). It was "before" everything else. The Greek concept of timelessness or eternity, which we share, was unknown to the writers of the Old Testament. They piled up the "long ago's" and the "before's" to convey its meaning. That is what this writer has done.

As an attribute of the living God, Wisdom participates in the Creation (vss. 24-31). The cosmological notions about natural history given here correspond to those prevalent throughout the Near East. As in Genesis 1:2, the primeval waters antedate everything else, and the earth is the bit of order enveloped by them. But as in Genesis, so here, God, as Creator, rules all of these and impresses them to serve his purpose.

The influence of the role of Wisdom in creation, "then I was beside him" (vs. 30), has been inestimable in the history of

Christian thought. At many times and in many ways there have
been attempts to dissociate God the Creator from God the Re-
deemer; but in emphasizing the role of the divine Wisdom in
creation—that same Wisdom which makes possible man's participation in the life and purpose of God—this discourse has
served to expose the error of such tendencies and to help maintain the meaning of the unity of God for Christian faith.

Wisdom, having issued her invitation and explained her status
in the being of God, issues a final appeal (vss. 32-36) to close
her sermon. Man can hear Wisdom in the instruction of the sages;
or, as we might put it, the Word of God can reach him through
the study of Scripture. And to "find" Wisdom is to find "life"
(vs. 35). Not something about God, but God himself is the real
gift: to know God is to participate in his life and to live in fellowship with him.

Lady Wisdom and Dame Folly (9:1-18)

We have had repeated evidence that for the sages there were
two influences everywhere at work in the world, two ways open
to man, and two invitations to which he must respond. One leads
to life, the other to death. Here, once again, these two are contrasted and symbolized by the two women, Wisdom and Folly.
In this chapter a paragraph is devoted to each, but these are separated by a brief unit (vss. 7-12) which is really extraneous to
this comparison. The two sharply contrasted word pictures on
Wisdom and Folly in verses 1-6 and 13-18 must originally have
been intended as two halves of a whole.

Elsewhere the divine Wisdom went out to men to preach to
them (1:20-33; 8:1-21). Here she invites men to the banquet of
life, a feast comparable to the Messianic banquet prominent in
the Jewish eschatological hope. She has built a "house" and hewn
out "seven pillars." In all probability this is a reminder of the universal and divine character of Wisdom. A palace or temple was a
building of cosmic significance; in ancient Canaan, gods were said
to dwell in heavenly palaces or temples. In Israel it was recognized that God could never be contained in this way, that the
whole world was his temple (I Kings 8:27-30); nevertheless,
Solomon did build a house for God to dwell in, and this Temple
in which he was "enthroned" (II Kings 19:15) was a sign and
reminder of the universe over which he ruled. The "seven pillars"

may be an allusion to this. In rabbinic traditions the cosmos is variously reported as resting on either seven or twelve pillars.

In this heavenly house Wisdom is the gracious hostess. Her banquet is ready and she has "set her table" with meat and mixed wine, food such as in Israel was served only at the great festivals of Passover and Booths which were intimations of the final Messianic banquet. The New Testament incorporates this meaning in the account of the institution of the Lord's Supper (Luke 22:15-18), so that the sacrament of Holy Communion becomes an eschatological celebration of the fulfillment of the Messianic hope in Jesus Christ.

While in this picture Wisdom remains in her palace, she does send out her maids to issue an invitation and this is issued to all, to the "simple" and to those "without sense." This anticipates the parable of the Marriage Feast told by Jesus (Matt. 22:2-10). Through these heralds she issues her invitation, "Come, eat of my bread" (vs. 5). It is all free; one is reminded of a similarly evangelical invitation in Isaiah 55:1-5, where God offers men the food of life "without money and without price." In Proverbs the divine Wisdom is the mediator of the gift; in the New Testament it is "Christ the power of God and the wisdom of God" (I Cor. 1:24).

In sharp contrast to Wisdom as hostess at the banquet of life is the scene provided by "the woman of folly" (a more literal translation of the Hebrew for "a foolish woman" in verse 13). She is loud (see 7:11) and noisy, shameless in her efforts to seduce men. She prepares no banquet; her "house" is a dive, to use a current term for it. With irony we are told that she invites the "simple" (vs. 16); the implication, of course, is that those who heed her show their simpleness thereby, not that she addresses only them! Her invitation, as that of the serpent in Eden (Gen. 3:4), no doubt appeals to the pride of those to whom she calls—something like today's "Learn what life is really like" slogans that accompany analogous solicitations. But all she has to offer is the food and drink of death. "Stolen water" is an intimation of adultery (see 5:15), though that particular sin is symbolic of all evil and, more to the point, of the satanic invitation to evil which is everywhere contending with the call of God in Wisdom.

This sketch of the sordid house of Folly in contrast to the elegant one of the palace of Wisdom inevitably raises the question, Why would anyone prefer it? Why would anyone choose death instead of life? This is very probably precisely the question the writer or editor wanted to raise by setting these scenes beside each other. It is, of course, the question that touches a perennial enigmatic aspect of our human experience, the fact of sin and moral obtuseness. Is it due to ignorance or to the result of disobedience? The Bible as a whole, and Christian faith, say it is the result of man's disobedience, as the story and doctrine of the Fall indicate. At first glance one has the impression that for Proverbs the propensity to folly and self-destruction in man is simply due to his ignorance. The sages seem to think that education will solve the problem. There is, of course, much truth in this; but this ironical treatment of Folly stands as a reminder that the sages were not wholly unaware of "the mystery of evil" expressed by the reluctance of men to heed the call to life and their apparent foolish readiness to throw themselves into the arms of death.

Verses 7-12 comprise a little section separating the portraits of Wisdom and Folly but not closely related to either. Like them, however, it assumes that there are always two classes of people in the world, those who live in "the fear of the LORD" (vs. 10) and those who do not. The separation of the sheep from the goats (Matt. 25:31-46) begins here and now. To try to teach a "scoffer" (vs. 7) is to ask for trouble; only those who know "the Holy One" are teachable. Men live by the Wisdom that is the gracious action of God (note the "me" in verse 11); or, as in Deuteronomy 8:3, by "everything that proceeds out of the mouth of the LORD" (see Matt. 4:4). Yet every man, wise or fool, is responsible for his own decision.

SECOND SECTION:
"THE PROVERBS OF SOLOMON"
Proverbs 10:1—22:16

In contrast to the relatively lengthy discourses in the first nine chapters of Proverbs, this section consists entirely of aphoristic couplets. These two-line units are complete in themselves; they are usually not ordered in terms of continuing themes but stand quite independently, each couplet by itself. Even when two or more successive proverbs deal more or less with the same subject (for example, 10:4-5) the connection seems incidental rather than organic. There is no logical continuity of thought. The arrangement of the proverbs in the apparently helter-skelter order in which we find them was probably influenced by such considerations as the repetition of words, rhyme, and various other types of assonance which can seldom be communicated in translation.

This commentary is not designed to treat such brief one-verse units as are here, but larger units under topical headings. In the chapters that follow, the biblical text does not provide a basis for such topical headings. A verse-by-verse commentary would lead to repetitiousness and redundancy. Hence, as a general rule some comment will be made which applies to the chapter as a whole, even though it is hardly a topical unit. In addition, where practicable, in each case there will be provided a somewhat extended comment on some feature of the wisdom material that seems to be prominent in the chapter, even though it appears elsewhere as well.

Proverbs 10:1-32

The Righteous

This chapter consists almost entirely (but see vss. 18, 26) of two-line couplets constructed as antithetical parallels, with the second line confirming the thought of the first by stating its opposite. Unlike folk wisdom of a proverbial sort, the sayings of the sages conform to literary forms that are rigidly fixed, much as are our sonnets. It has been proposed by some interpreters that these forms at one time originated in a cultic context, possibly as oracular sayings, but this is not now demonstrable.

In verse 7 "the memory of the righteous" is contrasted with "the name of the wicked." This is one of the very few instances in which Proverbs deals with the question of man's survival of death. The predominant view of the Old Testament is that at death a person goes to Sheol, the place of departed spirits. Here, amid gloom and purposelessness, they abide in weakness and inaction (see Isa. 14:3-11). This is the place to which all go, and all are treated alike. The "immortality" to which the Israelite looked forward was not this kind of half-existence in Sheol but the endurance of his "name" in Israel, especially in the clan to which he had belonged. A man's name survived, first of all, in the fact that he had descendants, and that they honored him. It lived on also in his deeds and accomplishments that were remem-

bered by the wider community. If the recollection of these continued to be a force for good in the era and circle in which they
were remembered, they were thought of as bestowing a "blessing." Such, says this proverb, is the name or the memory "of the
righteous."

Verse 26 is unusual in that the subject, "the sluggard," is compared to *two* other things, "vinegar" and "smoke." The structure
of this proverb does not conform to the forms for parallelistic
structure. One may surmise that we have here a "note for a
proverb" never worked up into its proper form.

The "righteous" are very prominent in all of Proverbs, and
nowhere more so than in this chapter. They stand over against
the wicked. These two groups are analogous to the wise and foolish, respectively; yet they are distinct from them. In the Psalms,
as well as elsewhere in the Old Testament, and especially in the
New, the righteous are sometimes equated with the poor and oppressed. In Matthew 6:2-4 and elsewhere, the reward of the righteous is no longer expected to be given them in this life. All of this
is different in Proverbs. Here the righteous is the man who does
the will of God as set forth by the sages. His deliverance is swift
and sure (11:8, 21; 12:13). Success (12:28; 13:21), wealth
(15:6), and honor (21:21) will come to him in this life. He does
not suffer hunger (10:3, 24; 13:25) and he escapes trouble (12:
21). The righteous will rule over the wicked (21:18; 29:16),
thanks to the goodness of God, and all men will rejoice in their
triumph (11:10; 14:34; 28:12; 29:2). They are like trees in a well-
watered garden (Ps. 1:3); "the root of the righteous will never be
moved" (12:3, 12). Their house stands (12:7), and their light
never goes out (13:9). Their good name and influence live on
after them (10:6-7). Many of these views about the righteous,
particularly about the swiftness of their reward in this life, are
challenged in the Book of Job. The result of this challenge was
that the nature of the rewards began to be redefined, and it was
seen that it was for God to decide when the rewards would be
granted. In the New Testament, "eternal life," a participation in
the life of God that transcends time, thus became the true reward
of the righteous. But Christian piety continues to treat temporal
success that flows from an observance of the will of God as a
token of this reward.

Proverbs 11:1-31

The Treacherous and the Blameless

As everywhere in this section, so in this chapter, each couplet stands by itself, and there is a large variety of themes. The very first one contrasts cunning, trickery, and deceit with sincerity, integrity, and blamelessness. To illustrate the difference between these, verse 1 uses the familiar market-place example of the scales: the "false balance" in contrast to the "just weight" (literally, the "complete stone"). In a society where weights and measures were not fully standardized and where the wide variety of devices could not be inspected and tested by official norms, cheating in weights was easy; even in our own day, despite fixed standards and official inspections, we read about ingenious devices by means of which the graduated and illuminated dial is made to show a tally that does not correspond to the weight of the purchase. What irritates the writers of these proverbs even more than the theft and dishonesty as such is the cunning involved in the act of stealing. The scale appears to be in balance, though false; the weight passes for what it is not. The trickery and the deceit fool men; but, say these proverbs, they are known to God. This is "the crookedness of the treacherous" that destroys them (vss. 3, 6, 21). The "blameless" (vss. 5, 20), in contrast, are not the naïve who do not know what one can "get away with" but are those who, despite their knowledge of the wily devices current and available, refuse to compromise the dictates of justice and truthfulness.

It is pertinent to remember that the wisdom movement flourished in the refined circles of the social and cultural elite. Gross acts of stealing and lying are rare in such circles; arrests for infractions of the law are quite infrequent. But it is precisely in these same circles that some give a great deal of thought to the devising of cunning ways to attain selfish ends by means which are technically legal but morally corrupt. In some respects the sages exhibit the timidity, casuistry, and paternalism one associates with the stratum of society to which they belonged. Nevertheless, these proverbs on treachery and blamelessness make very clear that the wise never confused truth and justice with conventional practices that were legally tolerated.

Speech

In Hebrew the term for "word" also means "act" or "deed."

A word is an act; it accomplishes something. The effect of a word once spoken can never be undone, whether it be for evil or good. The Word of God, of course, is supremely decisive (Isa. 40:8; 55:10-11). But human speech is also important; it is never thought of as neutral or meaningless; it takes the shape of either a blessing or a curse.

This general biblical understanding of the dynamic nature of speech the sages shared. Moreover, because the spoken word was the primary means for their communication and teaching, they took its implications very seriously. To know the occasion for speech and to know the time for silence is one way of saying what it means to be wise. Tongue, lips, and mouth—the instruments of speech—must be used but also disciplined. Wisdom has its source in the "mouth of God" (see 2:6); and this wisdom, which is simultaneously the divine Word (8:1-21), is mediated by the mouth of the sages (4:5; 5:7; 10:31). The "tongue of the wise" (15:2) gives knowledge; and the "lips of a king" are inspired (16:10). For good or ill, speech plays a decisive role. Words are "deep waters" (18:4), and they can be either as destructive as "sword thrusts" or the means of "healing" (12:18). The Letter of James in the New Testament has many affinities with the traditions of wisdom; prominent among these is its preoccupation with this awesome "little member," the tongue, which is "a fire" (James 3:1-12). The power of speech in fools and scoffers destroys (Prov. 6:12-14; 10:6, 14; 11:9, 13; 12:6; 22:14). The tongue may be "a tree of life" (15:4); but death as well as life is in its "power" (18:21). The prudent use of the mouth yields good fruit (10:20; 12:14; 13:2); but a man's word puts him under obligation (11:15; see 6:1-5). Therefore restraint in speech is inculcated (10:19; 11:12; 15:28; 17:28; 21:23). Only fools use the gift of speech indiscreetly (10:14; 15:2), or with a malicious purpose (6:12; 11:11, 13; 17:4). The scoffer and his "perverse tongue" will be "cut off," that is, destroyed (10:31).

Verses 9-14 give a series of allusions to the important but ambivalent role exercised by speech. The mouth of the godless can destroy the neighbor by insinuating an evil report; but the "shouts of gladness" uttered when the wicked are defeated are a proclamation of the divine justice. It is better to be silent than to gossip; the "talebearer" weakens the whole society by his act of speaking, but the "blessing" uttered by a good man restores it. Speech should be a participation in the Word of God, that is, in his action.

Proverbs 12:1-28

Permanence

This chapter opens with a reminder that, though it flourished among the privileged elite in the socio-economic structure, the wisdom movement is lean and stern in its insistence upon self-criticism. The man who says he loves knowledge—that is, an intimate awareness of the ways of life ordained by God—must show a desire for correction and criticism if his assertion is to be taken seriously. One's love of knowledge is no greater than one's love of correction. Yet this relentless "discipline" which will never let a man alone or permit him to settle down with a given set of values and practices is not designed to make him slavish. On the contrary, it is the way that leads to his fulfillment as a human being. The proverb alludes to this when it says that he who "hates reproof is stupid" by using a Hebrew term for "stupid" which means "brutish" or "animal-like."

At verse 3 there appears the first instance of a recurrent theme in this chapter (vss. 7, 12, 19) which has wide currency in the book as a whole and implies a central aspect of Old Testament faith. The proverb mixes metaphors in a curious way: the first line alludes to the founding of a house or a city, the second to the roots of a tree. A man cannot build his life on wickedness; but the righteous man is as permanent as a flourishing tree. The mixing of the metaphors (see also vs. 12) is probably due to the fondness of the sages for the metaphor of the tree to illustrate the career of the righteous; the building metaphor is very common throughout the Old Testament. Both are preoccupied with a concern for permanence which is historical and which, nevertheless, extends far beyond an individual human life.

For the Old Testament, and especially for Proverbs, fulfillment, or the Kingdom of God, is anticipated as a material and temporal actuality. In the Decalogue (Exod. 20:12) children are commanded to obey their parents "that your days may be long in the land." This implies that they will have a long and prosperous life as individuals, but its real meaning goes much further. What is meant is that they, living on in the generations that come after them, will be permanently established in the land. This is the viewpoint of these proverbs also. Elsewhere, under the impact of the thinking engendered by the Covenant which God had made with all of Israel, these notions of permanence were attached to the whole people and the Land of the Promise. Here the influence of the Covenant is not evident, and the emphasis is more individualized: a man is the founder of a family, likened to a house, a tree, a city, or a tower. Our age tends to put a premium upon mobility, both geographical and cultural; the writers of Proverbs held to more static views in seeking to assure the permanence of meaning and values. For us, paradoxically but very profoundly, permanence is possible only because of change. This is due, at least in part, to the Christian confession that the Kingdom of God is never exhausted in a given material and historical actuality, even though all such temporal actualities can be the instruments and bearers of it (Heb. 10:34; 13:14).

The Diligent Man

The sages are advocates of the strenuous life. In such matters as industry and frugality they set forth what is often described as "Puritan ethics." Verses 9, 11, and 24 of chapter 12 are all preoccupied with the virtue of diligence in contrast to sloth and neglect. The first two of these are especially noteworthy for the fact that they seem to endorse manual labor. In the wisdom tradition of Egypt this is not the case. The worker, especially the farmer, is looked upon as one who, because of his toil, can never become wise. This view is also found in Israel's wisdom tradition, especially in the writing of Jesus ben Sirach, though in a qualified way. The wisdom movement in Israel combines a respect for the dignity of labor with a firm attachment to an aristocratic theory of society. In this the sages were followed by their successors, the scribes and Pharisees.

The "diligent man" is literally the man whose hand is *sharp*; it grips the tool employed. In contrast we have the slack man, whose hand is limp because it is not employed. The two are contrasted in 10:4 and in 13:4 as well as here in verses 24 and 27. Hunger and poverty (10:4; 12:27; 13:4; 19:15; 21:5; 24:30-34) are the fate of the lazy. They become slaves (vs. 24); and their reputation is bad (10:26). The diligent man is sure to become wealthy and to exercise authority. The industrious woman has a fair name (31:27). Work brings results; mere talk adds up to nothing (14:23). The sages describe the "good life" in terms of the results that diligence brings.

In Proverbs the emphasis upon the virtue of industry and hard work is supported by the view that man can, by submission to the discipline of learning, discover the way of God for his life and ensure the outcome in terms of his material, temporal condition. This optimism about knowing the will of God and using it as a recipe for material prosperity is often shared by Christians. But it was not always maintained in Israel's wisdom movement; both Job and Ecclesiastes attest to this. Nor is it clearly reaffirmed in the New Testament, though diligence is a Christian virtue also.

Proverbs 13:1-25

The Subtleties of Life's Way

In its view of man the Bible stresses his responsibility. It is not unaware of his physical capacities and limitations. It is also quite aware of the important part intelligence and reason can play in ordering the course of his life. But more decisive than either of these is man's will. A man must choose and act; and in his choice and action, for or against the command of God, his destiny is determined. He is righteous or wicked, received or cast out, because of his volitional acts. To the modern mood, deeply influenced by the determining power of various impersonal and nonvolitional aspects of human existence, this stress upon the will sometimes seems unfair. For example, many social and psychological aberrations once called sins are now described as illness.

A superficial reading leaves one with the impression that Proverbs accepts this relentless insistence upon choice and decision, with its questionable assumptions about man's freedom, in much too cavalier a fashion—more so than any other part of the Bible. This may be true in the sense that the book displays no awareness of a doctrine of sin to complicate the role of the will. But it is not so true in terms of the modern mood which insists that every volitional act is to such a large extent predetermined by a total personal history in which the role played by the will seems negligible. This chapter gives clear evidence that the writers of Proverbs were by no means naïve in this respect; they were quite aware that the process by which a person's life was shaped was many-sided and complex and that it contained many subtle but decisive forces.

Verse 2 contrasts speech with violence. The good man develops a reputation through habits of prudent speech. Not a single act of will but a habitual pattern of action plus the society's assessment of this are involved. The fine lines of "acceptance" and "prestige" or "status" were as evident to this writer as to the modern social psychologists; not just the will but a whole complex of forces are involved, and most of these the "good man" must simply accept for what they are—conditions. As for the "treacherous," they have no will at all: only an appetite for "violence." When we speak of irrational "drives," instinctive or pathological, we deal with the same phenomena. A similar keen awareness of psychological torture is evident from verse 4a: the lazy man's craving nets him nothing; that is, laziness is a disease. The sluggard wants to attain precisely what he lacks the will to perform.

Verse 7 indicates that the sages had explored man's capacity for fantasy and illusion. This simulation of wealth and poverty is made possible by a circumventing of fact and reason that issues in a corruption of the will. One explanation of the tendency among the sages to assume that "fools" and "wicked" were incorrigible may be found in their awareness of the very decisive character of such irrational factors.

It must be noted, however, that the nonvolitional dimensions of life are not simply recognized for the decisive role they play in the fate of fools; they can come close to being decisive also for the wise. We see this in verse 12. The endless deferring of the expected and longed-for event paralyzes the mind; but a "desire" realized is a "tree of life." Whole chapters of life simply happen to one, whether they are desired or dreaded. A man's power of choice and will, which the sages concentrate on, must be exercised within the context of the boundaries marked off by the whole range of material, social, and psychic determinisms. The sages were as acutely aware of these as the moderns. It is quite unfair to describe Proverbs' account of the human situation as a "pollyanna" or "ostrich" version that shuts out what it finds disagreeable. Nevertheless, Proverbs retains the optimistic view that reason and will, properly trained and disciplined, can overcome the hazards in the human situation and so grasp the irreversible and impersonal processes of life that they will serve man's fulfillment rather than his extinction. The tragic vision of Job and the pathetic view of man implied in Ecclesiastes do not share this hope of the sages who wrote Proverbs. But it lives on in Jesus ben Sirach.

Proverbs 14:1-35

Wisdom and Folly

With the single exception of 14:1, the personification of Wisdom and Folly is limited to the first section (chs. 1-9) of Proverbs. It is not impossible that this one couplet prompted the more extensive comparison (9:1-6, 13-18). The margin of verse 1 indicates that the Hebrew text reads "wisdom of women." This would make the proverb refer to the industry and good sense ascribed to the ideal wife in chapter 31; that is, wisdom of women such as would be used to establish a home. It may have been such a thought that led to the introduction of the word "women." But it seems more logical to relate the intent of the proverb to the thought of chapter 9.

The theme of the proverb recurs in verse 3. The self-destruction of the fool is accomplished by his own talk; but "the lips of the wise" establish him. The "house" of wisdom consists of the lives of men who are wise. In verse 7 the advice to leave the presence of a fool (compare Ps. 1:1) expresses the oft-repeated concern of the sages to avoid the contamination of the good by the evil. The two groups are to be kept strictly separate. One is left with the impression that the regeneration of a fool is so highly improbable that it is not worth any risks. Insofar as the wisdom movement is busy with the direction and training of youth this may be defensible. But there was more to it than that. The separation of the wise from the fools led to a stratification of society into classes marked by conventional standards in which "better" and "worse"—both "Pharisee" and "publican," who were the New Testament exemplars of the wise and the fool—suffered from stagnation. We are familiar with how this phenomenon repeats itself over and over again, also, in the villages and towns of America. The maintenance of fixed customs is no guarantee for the preservation of the "righteous."

Sadness

In verses 10 and 13 we discover that the apparent optimism of the sages about life is tempered in yet another way. In these verses we get a rare look into the inner life and awareness of a teacher of wisdom. We catch him, so to speak, in a moment when he is not in the classroom expounding his doctrines about the rewards of discipline and wisdom, but when he is off duty, alone, and looking at himself in a "low" moment. In verse 10 the point seems to be that the human spirit, both in its anxiety and in its exuberance, suffers from but is also protected by an ineradicable isolation. There is a sense in which a man's life is "a long loneliness," so that he cannot communicate what is most real about himself, but can only talk to himself. But one gains the impression that for the sage this is not an unmitigated deprivation, that he turns his isolation into a "secret garden." In any case this fleeting exposure of the sage's self-conscious awareness demolishes many of the popular charges of superficiality made against him. This is even more true when we add the sensitive but rather pathetic disclosure of his spirit in verse 13. This confession that "the end of joy is grief" speaks about the transiency of all human achievements and the fleetingness of the satisfaction men derive from them. "The end of joy is grief"; life runs downhill. Here, for a moment, Proverbs sounds the minor key on which the great themes of Ecclesiastes are to be based. In terms of what he is or can do for himself man is a pathetic figure.

The Poor

There is always an ambivalence in the view of Proverbs about the poor. On the one hand it often considers poverty a result of laziness (see the comment on ch. 12). Yet here (vs. 31) we are told that oppression of the poor is an insult to God and that kindness to the poor is a way of showing God honor, thus anticipating the parable of the Last Judgment (Matt. 25:31-46). God rewards respect and care for the poor; it is a duty and a test of character (19:17; 22:9; 29:14). Yet the poor suffer from injustice (13:23), lack friends (19:4), invite hatred (19:7), so that, as here (vs. 20), even their neighbor, equally poor, dislikes them and likes the popular rich. One encounters no concerted effort to combat this perennial state of affairs the sages analyze so carefully. They do not ask their pupils to love the poor, only to be kind and just to them.

Self-Control

Verse 29 deals with the virtue of self-control. In the wisdom literature of ancient Egypt the contrast between the fools and the wise was stated in terms of the "hot" and the "silent" man, making endurance, patience, and self-control the central criteria of wisdom. In a great many instances in Proverbs, also, the Hebrew word for "heat" is used as the word for anger; and in at least one instance, restraint is expressed by the phrase "cool spirit" (17:27). The prudent avoid the short-tempered (22:24). As a source of folly, only jealousy is a match for anger (27:4). In invoking the virtues of restraint and self-control, as in so many other matters, the wisdom movement was simply endorsing a universally admired virtue and using it as a part of the discipline by which to further its own goals. Christianity does this also.

Proverbs 15:1-33

The LORD

It is an interesting fact that Proverbs uses Israel's personal name for the Deity almost exclusively. The general term, God, occurs only at 2:5, 17; 3:4; 25:2; 30:5, 9; and, dubiously, at 14:9 (see margin). For the rest, the proper noun, translated "the LORD," is used throughout. This is a striking fact which distinguishes this book from the rest of the canonical wisdom literature. Ecclesiastes never uses "the LORD"; and "God" predominates in Job. This feature is made more conspicuous by the fact that, like these other two, Proverbs does not explicitly recognize the particular Israelite religious tradition. We do not read in this book about the great historical acts of God, as at the Exodus and in the conquest of the Promised Land, in which he redeemed Israel and made his personal "name" known (Exod. 3:13-15; 6:2). Nor, for that matter, are there very explicit references to the national and cultic institutions and objects which depended heavily on the use of the personal name for their significance; for example, "the LORD's passover" (Exod. 12:11) or "the temple of the LORD" (Jer. 7:4).

It is quite useless to speculate about the reasons that led the
authors of Proverbs to choose "the LORD" as their favorite term
for the Deity despite their lack of interest in Israel's election tradition. The evidence for that is lacking. It is more promising to
explore the range of meaning they attached to the term.

We cannot rule out the possibility that the use of the "name"
by these sages carried with it their awareness of its role in Israel
and their explicit association with Israel's confession of faith in
the use of it. But it seems impossible to demonstrate this. The
writers of Proverbs are deeply impressed by the moral order of
life that seems to them to appear as an integral aspect of the law
of nature or the created order. One is easily tempted to describe
the search of the sages for wisdom as simply a systematic attempt
to discover the unchangeable moral laws that control the course
of a man's life and upon the knowledge and observance of which
the outcome of a man's life depends. If this were the whole of
it, the term "the LORD" could only serve them as a synonym for
this fixed structure with its moral dimensions, a metaphor for the
inert and static laws that decide man's fate. There can be no
doubt that the thought of the sages moves in this direction. Proverbs emphasizes law more than grace and measures life by human
performance rather than by the power of God to show mercy
and forgiveness. Yet it does not simply reduce "the LORD" to a
fixed form of laws. This is clearly evident in chapters 1-9, where
Wisdom's proclamation sets forth the prophetic and evangelical
Word of God (1:20-33; 8:1-21). It is not so evident in chapters
10-22, but a careful study of the use to which the "name" is put
shows that for these sages, too, the Deity was more than the
created order in its moral dimensions.

In chapters 15-16 the term "the LORD" occurs nineteen times.
This very heavy concentration is no doubt quite fortuitous, since
these couplet-length proverbs are not arranged according to a
topical scheme. But it does provide a convenient occasion to
examine the use to which the term is put.

There are passages in which "the LORD" is simply the Judge: he
rejects the way and thought of the wicked and his sacrifice (15:8,
9, 26); all scales are measured by the weights he possesses
(16:11). In such statements it is not impossible to see in "the
LORD" only a personified way of talking about natural laws that
have a moral character.

It is true, however, that "the LORD" is present within a man's

life and impulse as well as over against them: he weighs the
spirit (16:2); and while a man plans his way with his mind, the
overruling action of God directs his steps (16:9). It is more
difficult to ascribe such notions to a purely static norm. The
"eyes of the LORD" (15:3) watch everywhere; he even knows
what happens in the realm of the dead (15:11). To be sure,
the expression may be read as no more than a metaphor
for the thoroughness of divine judgment, but there are other
intimations of a more dynamic, active role for "the LORD."

In every situation there is an openness whose meaning is
locked in the divine mystery (16:33). Hence a man must
"commit" his work to God (16:3) in the confidence that he
will establish it (see Ps. 90:17). In this context "the fear of the
LORD" must be taken as the awareness of this mystery (15:16,
33). This is also true of the "prayer" in which the Lord delights
(15:8) and which he "hears" (15:29). It must be viewed as a
confession of faith in the goodness of God and in his power to
realize the meaning of man's life in his (God's) way. The dynamic character of God is illustrated by the old Israelite notion
that he destroys the proud and protects the weak (15:25), thus
upsetting all natural probabilities. We may conclude that these
sages adhere to a view of divine providence (16:4) in which the
Lord is sovereign over as well as immanent in his created world;
they sense a dynamic freedom in God that can never be capsuled
in discoverable structures or in human formulations, however
sage.

Proverbs 16:1-33

A Fountain of Life

To the one who has wisdom, it is "a fountain of life" (vs. 22).
In an arid country such as Canaan, water, especially the flowing
water of springs and fountains, was a metaphor for the source
of life. The vitality of nature was as enduring as the availability
of sweet water; as long as there were flowing springs there was
always the promise of a new crop. The fountain is the symbol
for the perpetuation and restoration of life.

Because of its role as a life-giving symbol in nature it became
a metaphor for human reproductive capacity. In Proverbs 5:18
a man's wife is described as his "fountain"; that is, she can give

him children and perpetuate his name. The bride in the Song of
Solomon (4:15) is similarly described as a fountain. In Psalm
68:26 a summons to praise God is addressed to all "who are of
Israel's fountain."

In this section of Proverbs, "fountain" as a metaphor for life
is applied to what we would call the life of the spirit. It is
important to note that the wisdom here designated as the fountain of man's life is a human thing, the teaching of the sages.
This is evident from the use of the term elsewhere: "the mouth
of the righteous is a fountain of life" (10:11; 18:4); so is "the
teaching of the wise" (13:14) and a man's "fear of the LORD"
(14:27). Finally, in 25:26 the implication is that a righteous
man who does not yield before evil is a fountain of life.

This section of Proverbs is by no means the only part of the
Bible that transforms "fountain" from a metaphor of natural
vitality and physical reproductive capacity into one of spiritual
life. The prophet Jeremiah describes God as "the fountain of
living waters" (Jer. 2:13) that Israel has forsaken (Jer. 17:13).
And in the eschatological vision of Zechariah we read (Zech.
13:1) of "a fountain opened" for David and Jerusalem, to
cleanse them from sin. In the Book of Revelation (Rev. 21:6)
it is proclaimed that this vision is fulfilled and the one sitting on
the throne says that he will give the "water of life" from the
"fountain."

Two features distinguish the prophetic use of the metaphor
from that of the sages. First, the sages seem to separate the
spiritual from the material in a way that the prophets do not.
When Jeremiah bemoans the fact that Israel has forsaken its
"fountain" he announces that this will result in the physical
destruction of his people; they will not simply be fools, they
will cease to be. Similarly, the restoration vision of Zechariah is
one of both spiritual and material re-establishment. The sages
do not seem to hold together the spiritual and material in such
an organic and dynamic manner.

The second distinction between the prophets and sages in their
use of the metaphor is even more important: for the prophets,
God himself is the fountain; for this section of Proverbs, the wise
themselves are the fountain. To be sure, they would readily have
admitted that their teaching was authoritative just because it
was the means by which God spoke and acted. Nevertheless, by
designating themselves and their published messages as the

fountain of life, the sages became so specific about the Word of God that they tended to circumscribe his freedom. The whole issue comes to a head once more in the conversation between Jesus and the Samaritan woman at Jacob's well (John 4:1-26). The Greek word for "well" literally means "fountain," and we may safely surmise that the story presupposes the Old Testament antecedents. God himself is the only fountain of life that continues to flow forever; there comes a time when even the lives and words of sages can no longer give life. Truly, "the well [literally, hole, pit] is deep"!

A Hoary Head

"A hoary head . . . is gained in a righteous life" (vs. 31). It seems that in most ancient societies great respect was attached to age. This was certainly the case in Israel, where the figures of the patriarchs and of "the elders in the gate" are the symbols of the continuity of the community and of its just government.

The wisdom movement has its own reason for stressing the accent upon age. In Proverbs, wisdom is the fruit of a long search. Study, observation, experimentation, practice, experience, and discipline all must play a role in its achievement. In a real sense only the aged can claim it. One is reminded of the great reverence attached to age in the Confucian traditions of China, traditions that have many affinities with those of the sages in Israel. Strength is the glory of youth (20:29) and should be admired for what it is; but for the sages the discipline of wisdom is more important than the power of the warrior. It must be remembered also that for Proverbs long life is a mark of divine favor.

Proverbs 17:1-28

Bribes

The two references to "bribes" in this chapter strike one as quite contradictory. In verse 8 bribery seems to be treated with approval, while in verse 23 it is a mark of the wicked man.

First it is to be noted that in verse 23 the man who accepts a bribe is wicked because he is prepared thereby "to pervert the ways of justice." In 15:27 we find the same attitude: those who hate bribes will live, as opposed to those who are "greedy for unjust gain." That is, the giving of gifts to influence legal decisions is bribery and is unconditionally condemned. This is the position of the Old Testament throughout. Deuteronomy 16:19 forbids the perversion of justice by the taking of a bribe; and the sons of Samuel were rejected because they disobeyed this commandment (I Sam. 8:3). Job echoes this law: "the tents of bribery," the homes and possessions of those who practice it, will be consumed by fire (Job 15:34). Since God accepts no bribe and executes justice for the poor and the widow (Deut. 10:17-18), all attempts to thrive on bribery—that is, on the accepting of gifts at the cost of justice for the innocent—must lead to a man's destruction. Only those who do not "take a bribe against the innocent" (Ps. 15:5) can hope to dwell in God's presence.

In the face of this, how is verse 8, which attributes prosperity to the one who gives a "bribe," to be interpreted? One is tempted to read it as a bit of sarcasm: the self-confident man of means making his way by crossing the palms of men whose co-operation he seeks is only preparing for his own destruction! While one could do this with this proverb, it is not clear that it is what should be done with it. The word "bribe" does occur with what is clearly an approved sense in 21:14; there it is a "gift" to put an end to violence. While the Hebrew word for "bribes" nearly always has the evil connotation of a payment to pervert justice, it can refer to a gift made with innocent intentions. In 6:35 it is translated by the English word "gifts" and refers to what we might call "hush money." The almost exclusively evil meaning of bribery associated with "gifts" from one public figure to another in Israelite society corresponds closely to the suspicion with which the public views "gifts" sometimes made to public officials by representatives of industry today.

Forgiveness

Forgiveness (vs. 9) has a very limited meaning and role in Proverbs. Here it is used as an aspect of human relationships. The basic meaning of the word used here is to "cover"; and in the other places in which it occurs, English words more closely approximating that meaning have been used: "conceals" (10:6, 11, 18); "keeps . . . hidden" (11:13); and "ignores" (12:16). The last of these meanings serves very well here also, for, as the second line of parallelism makes clear, the forgiveness consists in *not* "repeating" an offense, by talking about it or by retalia-

tion; that is, it should be ignored or hidden. Without intending
to depreciate the self-discipline and farsightedness of the man
who is lauded in verse 9, it is important to recognize that, despite
the use of the English "forgives," there is here no hint of an open
confrontation between offended and offender or of any explicit
reconciliation. We all know, in one way or another, that such
confrontations and reconciliations are only rarely possible in
human relations and that attempts to force them can lead to very
disastrous results. There can be no doubt that the counsel given
here, to ignore an offense, is a very salutary one; but it only
touches the edge of the biblical teaching about forgiveness. It
deals only with restraint and the absence of retaliation, not with
reconciling action.

In the Old Testament, God was also thought of as "covering
up," "concealing," or forgetting about man's offenses against
him. The Day of Atonement, still observed as the most solemn
day of penitence in the Hebrew calendar, reminds us of this: it
is called Yom Kippur (literally, the day of "covering up," or of
"propitiation"). This term also occurs in Proverbs: as "ransom"
in 13:8 and 21:18, and as "appease" in 16:14. In 16:6 we learn
that a man atones for (that is, "covers up") iniquity in the
human scene by "loyalty and faithfulness."

Proverbs teaches men to "ignore" and "cover up" the offenses
of their fellow men. It does not teach very explicitly that God
"ignores," "covers up," or "forgives" man's offenses against him.
Much less does it say anything about a reconciling action of God
in which he takes the initiative in seeking out and restoring to a
state of grace those who have rebelled against him and whom
he has punished, a theme so prominent in Isaiah 40-55. The
word for forgiveness or "pardon," connoting the reconciling
action of God and his initiative in grace, does not occur in
Proverbs. Nor does the verb "to have compassion" occur. This
verb is very common elsewhere in the Old Testament with God
as its subject and is used to describe the faithfulness and love
of God which move him to his reconciling act of forgiveness
expressed in renewal and restoration of the Covenant relationship. In a very serious sense, divine pardon and mercy are
inoperative in Proverbs. This seems to inhibit a profound understanding of forgiveness and compassion in the human social
scene as well. Forgiveness is seen as only the ignoring or suppression of evil.

Proverbs 18:1-24

The Haughty and the Humble

The Bible has an ambivalent attitude toward all human achievement and power. It thinks of it, positively, as means and sign of God's power; but also sees it as a temptation to idolatry and as a threat (18:12). Thus God chose Israel to make her great; but he must repeatedly break Israel when she becomes proud and forgets God. The power and the greatness belong to God, not to the man, nor to Israel.

This ambivalent view of human power opens the door to the possibility of socio-economic and political revolution. No particular order of things, however venerable or sacrosanct, is considered immutable or indispensable, although every order is a means by which God rules. The Bible does not directly inculcate the right of revolution as a human prerogative. It proclaims the freedom of God in relation to his world. The writers of the Bible illustrate this freedom by describing the great socio-economic and political reversals among men as evidence of the revolutionary character of the divine rule and judgment. God is the great Revolutionary in whose economy the first become last, and the last first. The so-called Song of Hannah in the Old Testament (I Sam. 2:1-10) and the Magnificat in the New Testament (Luke 1:46-55), which is an adapted paraphrase of it, are hymns celebrating the revolutionary character of God's rule.

It is interesting to see what Proverbs does with this theme. As might be expected, it deals with it entirely in terms of individuals rather than in terms of Israel as a corporate entity. This is clear from 18:12 and also from 16:18. Furthermore, the truth of the theme is maintained with reference to the dynamic character of God's rule expressed in judgment. The phenomena are treated more or less as an immanent law of nature.

As used in Proverbs, the two key words have a wide range of meaning: the "haughty" are those who hold high their eyes (6:17; 21:4), scorning those less fortunate than themselves; they have an exalted manner or "spirit" (16:18; 18:12); and they bristle with presumption (21:24). This adds up to a description of people who feel they are both self-sufficient and invulnerable. The "humble" are the retiring who do not push their influence (3:34; 11:2). They are people who are forced

down by need and affliction (18:12), or who lack the respect of
their fellow men (12:9). It is clear that humility, particularly,
is more than an inner attitude of either faith or resignation. It
refers to the brutal facts of deprivation and lack of recognition,
the status of a man which can only be altered by a reversal in
his *external* circumstances. It is quite remarkable that the sages,
in view of their social status and their very conservative tendencies, retained so much of the biblical realism in their thought
about the haughty and the humble. Specifically, they do not
treat humility as a religious or spiritual virtue wholly dissociated
from material circumstances, as tends to be the case in Christian
thought.

The Wife

The sages extolled the domestic virtues. A good wife was of
much greater value than material wealth (vs. 22). While they
admired the woman of talents (31:10-31), the significance and
meaning of all such gifts were measured by how they affected the
status of her husband. A good wife is "the crown" of her husband, and the one who brings shame on a man is "like rottenness
in his bones" (12:4).

Israelite society could not conceive of an independent role
for a woman: she was to fulfill her life in a husband who was
"known in the gates" (31:23) and in children who "call her
blessed" (31:28). The wife had hardly any legal rights of her
own; technically, before the law, she was the possession of her
husband. Even private vows made by her before marriage could
be voided by her husband, if he chose to do so (Num. 30:1-9).
The great respect accorded a faithful wife and mother by the
wise is all the more significant because of this legal distance
separating a woman from a man. Sons are admonished to obey
their mothers as well as their fathers, and the fool who causes
his mother grief is as sharply dealt with as the one who disgraces
his father (10:1; 15:20; 19:26; 20:20). Nevertheless, the wife
remains an accessory to her husband.

The sages seem to recognize a large element of uncertainty in
the choice of a good wife. She is described as a "favor" from the
Lord, a special sign of his good will (18:22; compare 19:14).
This seems to emphasize not only her great value, far greater than
wealth; but it also hints at the risks involved. The recipes for
wealth were more explicit and dependable than those for the good

wife. Proverbs makes it clear that a man unfortunate in his marriage is to be pitied above all others (12:4; 19:13; 21:9).

Proverbs 19:1-29

Poverty and Wealth

Poverty and the poor man were abhorrent to the spokesmen of the wisdom movement (vss. 4, 7). The wisdom movement represented an elite economic and cultural group. Its representatives were people who belonged to a leisure class; they were patricians who enjoyed inherited status and wealth. In Egypt many of the wisdom writings were preserved as "copy books" used by the young sons of the nobility. The maxims of the sages served as textbooks to teach the sons of the noble how to live successfully in the circle into which they were born. In Israel the situation was similar. The court of Solomon, deeply influenced by Egyptian royal styles, provided the initial momentum for the wisdom movement. As elsewhere in the Near East, literacy was limited to a rather small circle related to the Temple and the throne. The formal and systematic schooling of the young occurred only in this circle. In Israel the dissolution of the kingdom and the Exile no doubt created havoc for the movement; but it remained the prerogative of the elite and was finally merged with or transformed into the profession of the scribes represented early by Ezra (Ezra 7:6).

For the sages, the poor were people outside their own group. They knew them as people who had always lived in poverty or people who, because of their irresponsibility and profligacy, had fallen out of the circle of the respectable. The former probably evoked a distant feeling of sympathy; but the latter, their own "fallen brethren," must have filled the sages with revulsion. Those who were poor by inheritance could only be pitied. Through no fault of their own they were deprived of nearly everything that made life worth while. They had a claim on the kindness of those more fortunate (19:17). But the man who became poor because he squandered his resources deserved ostracism at the hands of his friends and brothers (19:4, 7). There appears also in chapter 14 (see comment) this ambivalent attitude of the sages toward the poor: they are poor because they have been disobedient, by being lazy or irresponsible. But one must remember that they are still creatures of God and be kind to them. It was much easier to be kind to those poor who had never belonged to one's own circle, and the widely differing spirit in the statements of the sages about the poor can in part be accounted for in this way.

However despicable or pitiable a poor man may be, he is to be preferred to a man "perverse in speech" (vs. 1); "a poor man is better than a liar" (vs. 22). Falsehood and lack of integrity are of the substance of wickedness and folly; poverty is only a symptom of them.

Wealth, we are told (vs. 14), is an inheritance from one's fathers—a notice that the sages belonged to a leisure class. But this wealth is to be husbanded with care, for the maintenance of one's freedom and leisure rests on it. Material goods as such are not the true goals of life; wisdom, "life," and "fear of the LORD" (22:4) are the real goals. But without wealth it becomes difficult to attain these. The sages invoke the advantages of wealth as an incentive to pursue the real goal they have in mind (12:27; 14:23; 21:17), just as the economic possibilities of certain vocations are used today to lure young men. In 19:4 there is the reminder that wealth brings "new friends," a doubtful blessing here counted as a plus.

Since wealth is only an incentive and by-product of the search for wisdom, the sages can, in principle, face the fact of its transiency without a qualm (11:4, 28; 23:4), even though the actual loss of it would fill them with utter dismay. They can and do condemn the passion for material wealth as a supreme good (10:2; 11:16; 13:11; 15:27). But they are quite realistic, and they are keenly aware that the possibilities for learning and culture do not exist apart from the availability of material support. It is important for modern Christians to see the truth of this: it is dangerous to speak as though goodness could exist apart from power, either in God or man. The sages' view of material wealth is much like that of the Old Testament as a whole; it should remind Christians that spiritual and material realities are inextricably bound together in this life and that they have a consequent responsibility for both.

Proverbs 20:1-30

Wine

In the days of the Old Testament, and again today, the Holy Land was a wine-producing country. Except for the special sect of the Rechabites (Jer. 35), the production and use of wine was considered a wholesome and useful enterprise. It was supposed to have been begun by Noah (Gen. 9:20). Everywhere in the Old Testament the presence of wine is a sign of blessing (Prov. 3:10); bread and wine rank with meat and milk as staples of life. We do not find evidence that there ever was a concerted effort to prohibit the production of wine as a staple commodity for general use. In Proverbs 9, verses 2 and 5, the personified divine Wisdom is said to have set her table with wine, just as the evangelical invitation in Isaiah 55:1 describes the grace of God freely given with the metaphors "wine and milk." To this day each Jewish Sabbath day is hallowed with wine; and at the Messianic banquet, as in the Lord's Supper, wine is the sign of fulfillment.

Though they honored wine, the writers of the Old Testament were alert to the risks it involved. Wine dulled the senses; hence it was useful for those in pain or at the point of death, but not for a king who must be alert to give clear judgment (31:1-9). It was also recognized that the use of wine lowered man's capacity for control, so that it could lead to violence (4:17). This is also the notion behind 20:1, with the added comment that wine is a "mocker"; that is, it scorns and ridicules its overindulgent user. Wine can easily destroy one's efficiency (21:17) and use up one's wealth. Proverbs (23:29-35) also contains a highly imaginative soliloquy about the man in a drunken stupor. It issues sharp warning to avoid the misuse of wine. Yet, though it is keenly aware of how easily such misuse occurs, and with what humiliating results, it assumes that wine plays an honorable and useful role in the human economy. It teaches temperance rather than abstinence.

The King

In its beginnings the wisdom movement had close ties with the king (20:2, 8, 26, 28). As a sacral figure he was thought to have access to the counsels of God, which were the ultimate source of all human wisdom; and he encouraged and provided for the schools that made the cultivation of wisdom possible and led to the production of a book such as Proverbs. Solomon was patron of the movement in Jerusalem, and 25:1 credits King Hezekiah with having continued it. Although the court in Jerusalem was destroyed in 587 B.C., and although the editing of Proverbs probably occurred after that, the book everywhere exalts the office of the king and inculcates the greatest respect for rulers. On earth nothing is more dreadful than the displeasure of the king (19:12; 20:2), while his favor is "like dew upon the grass." The king is God's instrument among men (21:1); the words he speaks in "decisions" (16:10) must be taken as God's word. It is as important to obey the king as it is to obey God (24:21). As the vicegerent of God he winnows and scatters evil, judging the wicked (20:8, 26) and rewarding the righteous (16:13; 22:11). It is recognized that a prince may act like a fool (17:7) and this degrades the office that should, above all, be exalted (19:10; 20:28). In the wisdom literature the king plays as central and exalted a role as does the priest in the literature of the Temple and its cultus.

Original Sin

The assertion implied in 20:9 that all men suffer from the impurity of sin seems especially noteworthy, since, in the Book of Job, it becomes a central means by which to defend the viewpoint of Proverbs that man can show that God is just. The dedicatory prayer in the Temple, attributed to Solomon, also makes the point that "there is no man who does not sin" (I Kings 8:46). It must be noted, however, that in neither case do we have an intimation of a doctrine of sin in the Pauline manner. Sin is not conceived as having destroyed the reliability and effectiveness of the human will; rather, the presence of sin, and of the tendency to it, must be countered by an alerting and disciplining of the will. For Proverbs, education is, throughout, by implication the answer to sin. Yet in verse 24 there is one more of the occasional expressions about the hiddenness of the way of man in God's plan which make it increasingly impossible to deal with sin in ledgerlike fashion.

Retaliation

In 20:22, Proverbs qualifies the standard Old Testament law of retaliation (Exod. 21:23-25). This parallels a growing development in the Israelite community as a whole. Those who transgressed the Law disobeyed God as well as doing injury to their fellow men. Similarly, the national enemies of Israel attacked God when they plundered his land. In both instances, by the law of vengeance and by the "holy war," respectively, it was initially incumbent upon Israel to right the wrong done to God. But gradually, partly because of the physical impotence of Israel, God was increasingly thought of as properly taking the initiative in these matters. Eventually, God alone will avenge himself and his people before the nations as a prelude to the final fulfillment of the promise (Isa. 63:1-6). And in the New Testament (Matt. 5:38-42) the law of retaliation is set aside.

Proverbs 21:1-31

The Weigher of Hearts

In ancient Egyptian religion there was a highly developed doctrine about the continuation of life after death. The building of pyramids, the practice of embalming, and the elaborate funerary rites were all related to this. One aspect of this doctrine related to the judgment after death to which a man was subjected. This judgment was carried out by a tribunal of the gods. All the dead man's deeds were reviewed. Some illustrations depict the weighing of the dead man or of his deeds in a pair of balances. The metaphor "the LORD weighs . . ." (21:2; compare 16:2; 24:12) occurs only in Proverbs. It seems fairly certain that Israel's sages took it over from those of Egypt. In Egypt certain gods weighed the hearts of men; for the Hebrew writers of Proverbs, the Lord weighed men's "hearts" or "spirits." It is important to notice that in using this metaphor, so intimately associated with Egyptian religious notions about a judgment after death, the Hebrew sages show no sign of having taken any of the religious ideas Egyptians associated with the metaphor. Like the prophets, they assume that God judges men in this life, and in taking over the Egyptian metaphor they simply make the point that he is aware of men's motives as well as of their acts.

Religion and Morality

Proverbs contains no explicit references to any of the institutions or forms of Israel's religious practice. There is no hint of circumcision, the Sabbath, or the dietary laws. The great festivals and their ceremonies are never alluded to; nor are the Covenant and the Ten Commandments. The relatively few references to religious practice that do occur are of such a general sort that they must have been equally intelligible to Israelite and non-

Israelite; just as today there are terms for universally held notions of a religious sort. The statements about sacrifice and justice fall in this class. The tie-up between religion and ethics is universal; and all sorts of religious traditions, ancient and modern, make the point that failure in conduct vitiates the meaning and effectiveness of rites and sacrifices.

In verse 3 moral obedience expressed in ethical conduct is said to be "more acceptable to the LORD than sacrifice." This statement and similar ones in the prophets (for example, Micah 6:6-8) can be taken in at least two different ways: (1) that ritual practice is optional or even dispensable, whether this be a sacrifice or the singing of a hymn; or (2) that acts of worship, though indispensable, must be rooted in a purity of motive which can be seen in ethical conduct. That Proverbs intends the second meaning is seen, first of all, in verse 27, which does not condemn sacrifice but the fact that an evil man brings it, and does so for the wrong reasons; and, finally, in 15:8, which tells us that God takes "delight" in the prayer of the upright though the sacrifice of the wicked is an abomination. The contrast is not between "sacrifice" and "prayer"; both are acts of ritual piety, and the parallelistic structure of the verse shows that they are to be treated as synonyms. The contrast is between the wicked and the upright, not between religion and ethics. This was also the point made by the prophets, though they dealt much more specifically than the sages with specifically Israelite religious rites and ethical standards.

Oil and Perfume

The sages who gave us Proverbs represented a cultural aristocracy; they had taste and they delighted in quality and elegance, but they detested ostentation (21:17). Oil was an indispensable requirement for a gentleman's toilet, just as his table was incomplete without good wine. The bath, completed with anointing and perfume, stimulated a valued lightheartedness (27:9; Eccles. 9:8) that made one more capable of facing the ambiguities of life. It was omitted on occasions of fasting and mourning, and its resumption marked the resumption of one's vocation (II Sam. 12:15-23). That is, oil and wine were not goods by themselves, much less means for vanity and display; they were important materials in the service of a total way of life. To use them apart from this context or without reference to it was to use them irresponsibly and objectionably. It may well be that Israel's sages were wiser than we in this matter.

Proverbs 22:1-16

Folk Wisdom

The section of Proverbs which began at 10:1 with the title "The proverbs of Solomon" ends with 22:16. All these chapters consist of two-line units. With very few exceptions these are couplets of parallelistic construction in which the second line repeats the idea of the first, whether antithetically or synonymously. This is clearly an "official" or recognized form of literary construction used by a professional group. Occasionally, however, we come upon a two-line unit which does not conform to this strict literary pattern. A good example of this sort of exception occurs in verse 13. This little story about the sluggard, whose excuse is humorous because of its improbability, does not follow any fixed literary form. Moreover, it corresponds to the sort of homespun folk wisdom not formally cultivated in schools and literary circles; it is proverbial wisdom of the sort that "just grew" rather than having been formally constructed, as in the case of the parallelistic couplets. This sort of proverbial folk wisdom is found in all cultures and nations and corresponds much more closely than the great bulk of Proverbs to what we usually mean by "proverbs."

THIRD SECTION
Proverbs 22:17—24:34

Thirty Sayings (22:17—24:22)

This section differs from the preceding one, first of all, in that it consists, in the main, of longer units. It may also be noted that like the first section (1:2-6), it is introduced by a lengthy preface giving the intention of the author (22:17-21). Also, like the first section, but unlike the second, it makes frequent use of the appellation "my son" (23:15, 19, 26; 24:13, 21).

What is perhaps most distinctive of this section, however, is the fact that its author or compiler has, in one section of it, made very specific use of a document of the Egyptian wisdom movement. In 1923 there occurred the first publication of an Egyptian papyrus document located in the British Museum. The title of this document is "The Instruction of Amen-em-opet." Amen-em-opet, the author of this "teaching of life," as he calls it, presents himself as a high state official in Egypt: the Overseer of the Soil or the Overseer of Grains and Provider of Foods. He says that he wrote it for his "son," the "Privy Councillor of Min Ka-Mutef." Expert opinion usually dates the manuscript in the seventh century B.C., though it is acknowledged that it may be older. The document consists of "thirty chapters" of the sort of prudent ethical counsel we associate with the Book of Proverbs. The first of these consists of a preface very similar in spirit and intent to the prefaces in Proverbs 1:2-6 and 22:17-21. The general affinity of this document with Hebrew wisdom in nature, form, and intent is clear.

But the 1923 publication of this document also showed that it had very much closer ties with this particular section of Proverbs. There is first of all the fact that in 22:20 the writer of this part of Proverbs says, "Have I not written for you thirty sayings . . . ?" What this seems to indicate is that he is using the Egyptian work of Amen-em-opet with its "thirty chapters" as his literary model; he wants to produce his own thirty-unit guide! Further, it was discovered that 22:17—23:11 consists almost entirely of a pastiche of phrases and lines drawn from various parts of the Egyptian document. From 23:12 to 24:22 this is no longer the case; whether these "chapters" were drawn from some other source, now still unknown to us, in a similar way we cannot say. It seems possible. But what is evident is that the writer of this section of Proverbs either had access to a copy of "The Instruction of Amen-em-opet," or knew it by heart, when he prepared his "thirty sayings." Attempts to reverse the dependence have not proved convincing. In any case, this dramatic discovery in literary history illustrates in a very concrete way the close ties and opportunities for exchange between the wisdom movements in Israel and Egypt. For Jews and Christians the Bible is the Word of God; it is, however, in its form and history, fully involved in and organically a part of the forces and processes of human existence in history. The Christian affirms the same about Jesus Christ in the Incarnation.

The Preface (22:17-21)

There is no complete agreement on how the author would have numbered his thirty sayings; for example, is this preface to count as the first? Is 23:12 by itself a saying? Or should it be combined with 23:13-14?

The fact that in this section the author is culling the Egyptian document for phrases does not result in a basic separation in spirit or outlook from other parts of Proverbs; there can be detected, however, a somewhat novel use of words and metaphors. For example, before the discovery of the document of Amen-em-opet, the meaning of 22:18 was always a puzzle: what was meant by keeping the words of the wise "within you" and also having them "ready on your lips"? Now it is clear that in this verse the writer was trying to condense the idea of several lines in the Preface of Amen-em-opet. What the latter said was that the keeping of the words of wisdom in one's heart or "belly" had the effect of providing the tongue with a mooring-stake, so that it would be silent when it was wise to be silent. It is now widely agreed that the Hebrew term translated "all of them" is really the term for "peg," so that the second half of the verse should be read, "if as a peg they are ready [or fixed] on your lips"; that is, to keep the tongue tied up.

Verse 19 is another instance in which the discovery that this author used the Egyptian document helps us to recover his meaning. In Egyptian wisdom "the way of God" corresponds to "the fear of God" among Israel's sages. The Greek version of this verse reads "his ways" instead of "even to you" to conclude the verse. Thus, very probably the second line of verse 19 should read, "I have made known to you today his ways." This relates it much more significantly to the first line.

The term "written" (vs. 20) occurs only here in Proverbs. This must also be related to the fact that the writer depended on an Egyptian and, possibly, other documents. Originally, the sages composed these proverbs orally; this man comes closer to being an anthologist or commentator than an author. He depends on written sources and produces a document; his work does not pass through a stage of oral circulation and transmission as was true of such material as we find in 10:1—22:16. This man is an early example of the "scribe" who became very prominent in later Judaism and played such a great role in the production of postcanonical Jewish writings, notably the Talmud. His primary function is that of a commentator who does his work in writing. In Psalm 45:1 the poet says that his tongue is like the pen of a "ready scribe"; and Ezra (7:6) is described as a "skilled" or "ready" scribe. The term "ready" (literally, quick, apt) connotes the professional circle to which this sage belonged; he, too, was "skilful [the same Hebrew term is used as in Psalm 45:1 and Ezra 7:6] in his work" (22:29) as a scribe who was a commentator on wisdom.

Five "Chapters" (22:22-29)

These five "chapters" (vss. 22-23, 24-25, 26-27, 28, 29) show that the writer's use of Egyptian materials does not turn him aside from the favorite subjects of Israel's sages. The obligation to protect the poor, with its reminder of the vengeance of God upon their despoilers (see Exod. 22:21-24), the warning against giving pledges (see the comment on 6:1-5), and the warning against the removal of the landmark (see 23:10-11) are common in Israelite circles. It may be noted, however, that the last of these is given prominence in Amen-em-opet also and is not dealt with in other sections of Proverbs, so that this writer is probably prompted to use it because of his Egyptian source rather than because it figures in Israelite law (Deut. 19:14).

Five Other "Chapters" (23:1-11)

These eleven verses conclude the part of this section that has made direct use of Amen-em-opet. There are five "chapters" or "sayings." The last of these, relating to the landmark, is similar to 22:28. The first three of the others also show clear evidence of Egyptian influence.

Although social etiquette, with specific reference to table manners, became an important preoccupation in later stages of Israel's wisdom movement, Proverbs does not become very explicit about it. In this section (vss. 1-3) it is not clear whether the purpose is to develop self-control and good manners or to inculcate a healthy suspicion of the ruler who acts as host. This note of suspicion and warning seems even stronger in Amen-em-opet's treatment of the subject: the possibility that the host may want to secure secrets, or even to poison his guest, is suggested. If these verses are indeed, as we feel, a warning against craftiness, rather than a reminder about good manners, their subject was almost certainly suggested by the Egyptian document. That sort of thing is not common in Proverbs. Much later, in certain rabbinic sayings from about the era of the New Testament, we do find a similar sentiment: "Be careful with the government, for they do not come near to a man except for their own need."

The second unit (vss. 4-5) is a reminder of the transiency of riches. This corresponds to the spirit of Ecclesiastes rather than to that of Proverbs. The matter is treated in precisely the same spirit by Amen-em-opet. He stresses the transiency both of human life and of riches. The last two lines of verse 5, dealing with the transiency of riches, are based on the Egyptian lines which describe wealth as having made itself "wings like geese" and having flown away to the heavens. In the Hebrew version, however, the eagle, the bird of the mountains, has displaced the water bird.

The unit on the calculating host (vss. 6-8) has much in common with the first in this chapter. He is a host either because custom demands it or because he has evil designs of his own. As verse 8 indicates, the guest will leave with a bad taste in his mouth.

On the Training of Youth (23:12-28)

Verses 12-16 consist of three separate units, all related to the training of the young. In verse 12 there is a reiteration of the oft-repeated admonition that there is no short cut to learning and wisdom: education is mainly a matter of application. The next unit reinforces the importance of this by advocating the use of corporal punishment as a means of achieving it (vss. 13-14). A beating will not kill the son, or pupil; it will save him from the sort of foolishness which is no better than death (Sheol). This is said by an old-fashioned schoolmaster whose motto is "Spare the rod and spoil the child." In the third unit (vss. 15-16) the teacher says that the real reward of his profession is in the product he turns out; if his pupil begins to show the marks of a truly educated man, the master will rejoice. If this is also the authentic spirit of the master who resorts to corporal punishment, any evil effects of it might perhaps be deflected. Verses 23-25 can well be read as a reiteration of the first and third units dealt with here.

The Drunkard (23:29-35)

Proverbs indicates a carefully reasoned attitude toward the

use of wine (20:1, see comment). Here we have what amounts
to a literary "skit" to portray those who are ignorant of or flout
the counsel of the sages in this matter. It is a warning against
drunkenness (vss. 29-32), reinforced by a mockery of the
drunkard (vss. 33-35). A sixfold rhetorical question introduces
the subject; the fate of the drunkard is summed up in the range
of the questions: personal, psychic, social, and physical disaster
strikes those who "tarry long over wine." Wine in Israel was a
sign of the blessing of God and was to be used as a way of exem-
plifying the meaning of this blessing in every activity and depart-
ment of life. To make it an end in itself, and simply a means of
self-indulgence, was to invite the disasters that afflict the drunkard.
Wine must assist one in living life; to use it as an escape from
the living of life was to make it an enemy.

The highly realistic description of the stupor of the drunkard
is heightened by the use of the second person: "you," "your."
The uncertain gait of the drunkard—or the sensation he experiences as he lies in a stupor—is compared to the rolling of
the sea. In the Greek version (Septuagint) verse 34b reads,
"Like a steersman in a great storm." The mockery ends with
the reaction of a confirmed addict who wants to start over
again.

Wisdom and Constructive Power (24:1-9)

This little group of four "sayings" is loosely held together by
the contrast between wickedness or folly and wisdom as resources
for constructive action. Wisdom makes it possible to build a
house (vs. 3). "House" here is symbolic of a creative purpose
to be achieved in the attainment of a goal. Just as God created
the earth and the world by means of Wisdom (3:19; 8:22-31),
thus realizing his intention, so a man can use his wisdom to do
likewise; he will build his "house." The metaphor is continued
in verse 4: by "knowledge" every room of the house will be
filled with beauty and treasure. That is, any worthy project for
which one invokes wisdom can be fully achieved; there will be
no loose ends. The following saying (vss. 5-7), which states that
the wise is mightier than the strong, comes as the sequel one
might expect if wisdom rather than brute power is the effective
resource for every enterprise. This comparison of disciplined intelligence and material strength is found in many cultures. To
wage victorious war, men and matériel are not enough; it

demands "wise guidance" (literally, "tactics") which only trained
and disciplined intelligence can provide. Brains matter more
than brawn. In contrast to the constructive potential of wisdom,
evil and folly are the resources for negation and destruction
(vss. 8-9).

Moral Courage (24:10-12)

This is a remarkable passage. It advocates overt action, to be
taken at great risk, in a situation in which this could presumably
be avoided. In the "day of adversity," when your neighbors are
in trouble, to "faint" (literally, "relax"), to do nothing because
you want to be safe, is to display a lack of courage and manhood
that neither men nor God can condone. We are reminded in
verse 11 that throughout the centuries and the millennia Jews
have, over and over again, been subjected to sudden violent
attacks involving deportation and death. The bloody pogrom
and the midnight call of the police were well known to the Jews
in the day of Proverbs. In the day of such raids one's courage
and manhood are put to the test: does one dare to rescue those
being led away or to conceal intended victims? Some will cover
up cowardice or indifference with the excuse that they did not
know what was happening: "Behold, we did not know this." This
excuse, apparently offered twenty-five hundred years ago, figures
prominently and perfidiously in contemporary history. In the
era of National Socialism in Germany, from 1933 to 1945, six
million Jews were taken away to their death; and at the end of this
period the almost universal excuse was, "We just did not know
what was happening." But such veiling of indifference, com-
plicity, or cowardice will not avail: God who "weighs the heart"
and is the keeper of your life knows why you failed.

Prudence and Composure (24:13-22)

The call to overt action involving great risks occurs infre-
quently. More common is the advocacy of contemplativeness,
dignity, withdrawal from or indifference to popular moods, and
prudence in conduct. These are the themes that predominate in
this series. The fare of wisdom is good food, like honey (vss. 13-
14); wisdom and learning secure one's future. Avoid the folly
of attacking the righteous (vss. 15-16). To rejoice at the fall of
one's enemy is to invite God's displeasure: God sends him to
his fall, and for a man to gloat over this is not only to act with-

out dignity but is to invite the divine judgment upon himself
(vss. 17-18). To become agitated about the success or threat
of the wicked is to show a lack of faith (vss. 19-20). Be on good
terms with God and the king (vss. 21-22); they have authority
over your life. To disobey them is to disobey the truth and also
to lay one's self open to reprisal. Be prudent. The sages knew
how to combine principle with calculation!

A Supplement (24:23-34)

The four brief paragraphs that make up this supplement are
quite similar in form and subject matter to the preceding "thirty
sayings" (22:20). But in verse 23 the editor of Proverbs, or the
author-compiler of the "thirty," recognizes them as a separate
part, a supplement.

The sages, along with the legal writers and the prophets, consider the maintenance of the integrity of the judicial system of
central importance (vss. 23-26). To call the wicked innocent, in
official testimony or unofficially, for whatever reason, is to invite
the curse of mankind (vs. 24). The Letter of James (2:9) summarizes the intent of this saying: "If you show partiality, you
commit sin."

In the Old Testament, "house" can mean "family." To build
a house (vs. 27) can mean to found a family, and this is probably
the meaning intended here. The counsel given here is that those
who contemplate marriage and a family should prepare for its
maintenance beforehand.

One may not bring a groundless charge against one's neighbor,
not even to retaliate for his having done so. In verse 29 we have
a negative version of the Golden Rule (see 20:22). If obeyed,
the negative command does not initiate a chain reaction of good
will, but it does break a chain reaction of vengeance and retaliation which clears the way for good will.

Verses 30-34 contain a story with a moral. The sage takes a
walk to the farm of the lazy man. He shakes his head at what he
sees and composes a lesson. Elsewhere (6:6) he advised the
sluggard to take a trip to the ant heap, so that he might also
compose a story. Unfortunately, it seems that he never did.

FOURTH SECTION:
THE COLLECTION OF HEZEKIAH
Proverbs 25:1—29:27

Preface (25:1)

The note at the beginning of this section states that its contents
are proverbs "copied" by "the men of Hezekiah king of Judah."
The era of Hezekiah was one in which, at least for a time, the
crushing suppression of Assyrian domination was lifted. This
must have made it easier to establish contact with the other great
center of political power, Egypt. It has been suggested that the
era of Hezekiah was the one in which active interchange between
the wisdom movement in Israel and the legacy of wisdom in
Egypt, exemplified by the preceding section, began. The note
does give hint at a revival of the work of the sages in Hezekiah's day.
It also reminds us that they enjoyed royal patronage and that
the activity of coining and copying proverbs was a perennial
process—the work of a movement, not just of occasional individuals. The copying was, of course, intended to preserve the lore
of the past; as in Egypt, it may also have played a role in the
instruction of the current crop of pupils.

The section consists of two parts, 25:2—27:22 and 28:1—
29:27. These are separated by a brief discourse on grazing as a
way of life (27:23-27). In the first part the literary form is more
complex than was true in the Second Section (10:1—22:16).
There are quatrains as well as couplets; and sometimes they are
combined to provide a more lengthy treatment of a particular
topic. Antithetic parallelism, common in chapters 10-15, is rare
in this part. The second part, on the other hand, consists mostly
of couplets; and they are mainly of the antithetical variety.

The Collection of Hezekiah: Part One (25:2—27:22)

Examples of Etiquette and Grace (25:2-14)

In 25:2-7b two couplets and two quatrains are tied together
by the fact that all four make a reference to the "king"; the
word as such, rather than any continuing idea, ties them together.

The king himself is the subject of the couplets; he is viewed with boundless enthusiasm and awe (see ch. 20). It is the "glory" of kings to "search things out"; that is, to be great sages. The philosopher-king ideal is extolled. Ideally the king should actually be the greatest sage in a society, as well as the patron of them all. His wisdom and authority combine to make him inscrutable. The two quatrains have aspects of the king's environment as their subject. The brilliance of a reign depends on the removal of the dross. The admonition to be extremely modest in the presence of royalty parallels frequent Egyptian reminders of the same sort. The saying, "it is better to be told, 'Come up here,' " no doubt served as the seed for Jesus' parable about status in the Kingdom of God (Luke 14:7-11).

Verses 7c-10 caution against bringing against a neighbor charges that cannot be substantiated. Great weight is attached to the shame and humiliation one would bring upon one's self if the untenability of one's charges were exposed and if the one against whom they were made decided to exploit one's own failings. The really constructive proposal is to have the matter out privately with one's neighbor and avoid the official judicial machinery as much as possible. This sort of counsel became increasingly common in later Judaism and is enjoined in the Sermon on the Mount (Matt. 5:25-26).

The right word at the right time; to know what to say and how to say it: such is the test of wisdom, and it is a gift that cannot be overvalued (vss. 11-12). He who has it turns reproof into a constructive experience.

Ice-cold water refreshes the parched harvesters in the heat of summer. A messenger upon whom one can depend brings the same sort of refreshment. The courier played a prominent role in Israelite society; he carried confidential messages by word of mouth, as well as valuables and secret documents (vs. 13). In a land always on the edge of drought nothing is as disappointing as the promise of rain that does not materialize; so are those who promise gifts but do not deliver them (vs. 14).

A Dozen Proverbs (25:15-28)

The last half of the chapter consists of a dozen proverbs essentially unrelated to one another. In some cases the sequence is determined by catchwords, but this cannot be shown in translation. Patience, moderation, integrity, and self-control are prominent themes. The advice to feed one's enemy (vs. 21) gave Paul a cue for his counsel on Christian conduct (Rom. 12:20). Verse 28 is a graphic metaphor dealing with the oft-repeated concern for self-control (see ch. 14).

Portrait of a Fool (26:1-12)

With the exception of verse 2, this is a series of couplets all dealing with the fool. They are not really organically related to each other, nor do they represent progressive thinking about the subject. The term "fool" is the only thing that ties them together. Each can be used entirely by itself. The effect is similar to that created when a large series of headlines from many newspapers, or snapshots all dealing with the same subject, are printed or mounted helter-skelter on a single page in the fashion of a collage. The total creates an impression all its own.

In verses 4-5 two apparently contradictory bits of advice are set in juxtaposition. On the one hand, the sage must refuse to meet the fool on his own level; to treat him as an intellectual or moral equal is out of the question. On the other hand, the inanities uttered by the fool must be refuted and the fool must be exposed for what he is. The lines of class distinction are sharply drawn here: the fool must be kept in his place, and those who keep him there must avoid contamination.

Verse 7 reminds us that for the sages, proverbs were not a matter of rote learning; they were material for the shaping of lives and of human character. Therefore, a fool's recitation of a proverb has no effective result: it can no longer change his character, any more than a lame man's legs permit him to walk.

Verses 8-10 show that fools were often considered worse than useless; they could be a menace. To show respect to a fool (vs. 8) or to give him power (vs. 10) is to ask for trouble. The fool will use the "stone in the sling" to injure the one who put it there; and the man who employs a fool, giving him tools and authority, makes life unsafe for all his neighbors.

Verse 2 is unrelated to this series on the fool. It is not possible to say why it is found here. What it says is that the words of a curse need not be feared unless they are based on something that is true about the person or object cursed. The curse was taken very seriously in ancient Israel, as in some lands today. There was often the belief or dread that a mere utterance of a curse effected what was intended. Here, and elsewhere, we are reminded that a curse is made effective by the action of God, not simply by a human utterance of words. In the last analysis, only God can curse a man or a situation.

Portrait of a Lazy Man (26:13-16)

Again independent proverbs are tied together by a single word, in this case, "sluggard." The result adds up to a mordant and bitter humor that holds the lazy man up to contempt. The first and third "stories" create amusement because they are so unlikely: lions keep to the mountainous wilderness, as everyone knows; and who ever heard of a man too lazy to eat? But the second picture (vs. 14) evokes exasperation: what is harder to endure than the sound of a door endlessly swinging on a squeaky hinge? The exasperation is completed by the impatience produced by the hopelessness of the situation in verse 16; the lazy man is beyond counsel!

Quarreling (26:17-21)

The sages were experts in the psychology of human relations. Prudence and composure (see ch. 24) rather than impetuosity described their ideal. Insofar as it accorded with their sense of communal responsibility and moral courage they sought to live above life's passing scene. And when they felt compelled to interfere with it they sought to do so with forethought. Callow humor, that does not consider the possible misinterpretation to which it is open, is to be avoided (vss. 18-19). No matter how innocently intended, these thoughtless attempts at "fun" leave irreparable damage. In trying to distinguish the fine line that separates responsible involvement from meddling, the sages were on the side of restraint.

The Schemer (26:22-28)

Duplicity of speech, the planting of rumors, gossip, flattery, and the masking of evil intentions are an abomination to all who love wisdom and want to be upright. The wise react to all of these as to something slimy. But much as they detest it all on moral grounds, and keenly aware as they are of the ruin it produces in a society (vs. 28), their most explicit reason for rejecting the schemer's tactics is their belief that they will fail. The evil purposes will be exposed (vs. 26), and the schemer will be overwhelmed by the evil he planned for others (vs. 27). This is the theme written into the Haman-Mordecai story in the Book of Esther.

The Transiency of Life (27:1-22)

Proverbs is largely optimistic about the possibilities of human life. In contrast to Ecclesiastes or Job, it believes there are a great many things man can count on, notably the material and historical rewards of obedience to God and the sages. Yet the book remains modest about man's power; he must live in the fear of God, knowing that not all of the mystery of God's way is disclosed to man. This chapter provides forceful reminders that the sages were acutely conscious of the brevity and transiency of life and of the endlessness of the quest of man for understanding. There are intimations here of the sentiments later expressed more fully in Psalm 90, which is also a product of the wisdom movement.

In verse 1 we have a reminder that the future, even tomorrow, is in the hands of God. No man knows what it will bring, or even whether he will live to see it. This should evoke that spirit of modesty and humility known in Proverbs as "the fear of the LORD." In I Kings 20:11, King Ahab quotes an old proverb to be relayed to the king of Syria: "Let not him that girds on his armor boast himself as he that puts it off," which says some of the same things intended by this verse in Proverbs. Yet there is more here: man's basic lack of control over his own world. Even the king returning triumphantly and boasting about the battle as he takes off his armor is confronted by the uncertainty of life. The parable of the Rich Fool (Luke 12:16-21) works with the theme of this verse. And the Letter of James (James 4:13-16) gives a very good exposition of it.

The transiency of man's life is further complicated by the fact that his search for meaning never ends. This is the burden of verse 20. Just as the realm of the dead, Sheol or Abaddon, is always asking for more lives, so man's search for meaning never ceases. There is always more to discover, more to analyze, and more to make sense of. Humanly speaking, the answers are never complete. The uncertainty of life and the incompleteness of it re-enforce each other, and together they should keep men humble.

Verses 15-16 are a striking example of the way in which the wisdom movement recognized the decisive role of a wife in the career of a man (see 18:22). Because of the importance of her role in a man's life, an unhelpful and nagging wife becomes his greatest liability. The worst thing about it, say these verses, is that there is nothing one can do with or about a woman or wife who wants to argue, carp, or complain (compare 19:13). It would be better to live in complete isolation (21:19; 25:24), like a hermit in the desert, than to be driven to distraction by the endlessly repeated complaints.

The Parable of the Shepherd (27:23-27)

To prosper, a shepherd must work with foresight. He must know his herd's condition, and plan for it in relation to the seasons, grass, gathered herbage, and new growth. Only a flock well managed and well planned for can be counted on to support the economy with clothing, food, and cash. This, it seems, is not just a lesson for shepherds but a parable about all of life, as verse 24 makes clear; the things entrusted to one, for one's use, do not take care of themselves. They require responsible attention if they are to yield their intended results. Man must live as a responsible steward. A farmer's parable in Isaiah 28:23-29 gives another example of the use of familiar scenes and practices to illustrate general issues.

The Collection of Hezekiah: Part Two (28:1—29:27)

The second part of the section consisting of the Proverbs of Solomon copied by "the men of Hezekiah king of Judah" resembles the large Second Section (10:1—22:16) even more than does the first. This is evident from the fact that it consists entirely of couplets predominantly constructed in the pattern of antithetical parallelism. It may also be noted that virtually the whole range of themes dealt with in the larger section recur again here and are handled in a similar way, so that the outlook on life appears to be the same in both cases.

Law and Justice

In the Old Testament the cry for justice is properly associated with the prophets, especially with Amos. The Book of Deuteronomy consists mainly of exhortations to execute justice, the Law being treated as the means and guide for this. Proverbs makes the same emphasis (see 28:4, 5, 7, 9; 29:4). In Israel justice consisted in the application of established precedents and custom to each new situation. Each application involved some measure of choice by the individual doing so. In this freedom an Israelite was to take into account and be guided by the spirit of the Law as a whole, making that his norm in applying the particular commandment to the issue at stake. Men with evil purposes would be so blinded by their own aims that they could not "understand justice" (28:5); that is, they did not understand what the Law as a whole indicated as right in a given situation. They might formally keep the Law and yet break it. Seeking the Lord included the desire to grasp this "spirit" of the Law. Whether in these proverbs "law" refers to the official Law of Moses is not certain. The sages also referred to their own instruction as law (*torah*); and single admonitions were called commandments (6:20, 23; 13:13; 19:16). While the sages had a much more man-centered view about the source and growth of law than the Pentateuch or the Prophets, the content of their instruction coincided closely with that of the Mosaic Law, as a comparison of Proverbs and Deuteronomy will show.

The Oppressor

The sages had an ambivalent attitude toward the poor (see comment on ch. 14). Poverty was no virtue and might be a sign of sin (see comment on ch. 19), but the poor were to be protected. This call for protection of the poor was based on the broad principle that it is wrong for any man to oppress another. Oppressors are driven by need or by the greed for power. In 28:3 there is the psychologically astute observation that the oppression of a poor man by a poor man can be the most devastating; the poor oppressor is driven by both need and greed. Like the Old Testament as a whole (Exod. 22:25; Deut. 23:19-20; Ps. 15:5), Proverbs holds that to charge interest is a form of oppression (28:8). Treachery is a form of oppression that will eventually overtake its perpetrators (28:10). Rulers are dangerous as oppressors (28:15, 16) because they possess power; the poor are the first to feel their heavy hand. Hatred of unjust gain is a mark of "understanding"; that is, of the knowledge of God and his law. The hungry and the hoarder (28:21, 22, 25) are driven to oppression by their inordinate need or desire. The man who robs his parents (28:24) is an oppressor of a special sort. In

Israel, property belongs to the family rather than to the individual; this may explain the excuse that this sort of dispossession constituted "no transgression." There may have been no laws preventing a son's utilization of the common estate for his own purposes at the expense of his parents. A close parallel to 29:13 is found in 22:2. The oppressor seems to have the advantage over the poor; but both have the gift of life, "light to the eyes," from the same God. He sees and judges both, and his judgment falls upon the oppressor.

Wisdom and Worship

Those who refuse to hear the "law" (28:9), whether the Law of Moses or the teachings of the wise, fail also in the realm of prayer. Intellectual effort and moral seriousness are prerequisites for worship.

The cultic seriousness of bloodguiltiness, well-attested elsewhere in the Old Testament, is set forth solemnly in 28:17. To help such a man, by touching him or accepting him in one's social circle, is to incur a share in his guilt; he must remain "a fugitive until death," as Cain was (Gen. 4:10-16).

In 29:18 "prophecy" is compared to "law" in a manner that seems to attach greater importance to the latter (see 28:9). The word translated "prophecy" means "vision," rather than "word" or "utterance" which are also used of prophetic oracles, and it may refer to some form of cultic divination or dream vision. This would emphasize the contrast with the keeping of the Law that seems intended here. That the effect of prophecy is wholesome is admitted, but keeping the Law is finally more important. The wisdom movement contributed greatly to later rabbinic Judaism in respect to the importance it attached to keeping the Law. But it is important to remember that it intended this inductively: men must seek to know the way of God, not simply keep rules.

Discipline

The discipline of a son is dealt with in 29:15 and 17, that of a servant or slave in 29:19 and 21. Both seem severe, and the latter seems to do violence to respect for personality. Corporal punishment of sons and pupils in Israel was coupled with great love and devotion toward them. This probably reduced the harm it did. But it is clear from 29:19 and 21 that the attitude to the servant was a very different one. He was under suspicion of being willfully intractable—"though he understands, he will not give heed"—and waiting for a chance to take over. This suspicion and fear dictated the treatment of the servant.

FIFTH SECTION: FOUR APPENDICES
Proverbs 30:1—31:31

The last two chapters of the Book of Proverbs consist of four quite independent units, each with a distinct character of its own, all of which were probably added to the main part of the book by its final editors or compilers. Their role in the book corresponds to that of an appendix or excursus in a modern book.

The Words of Agur (30:1-4)

The proper nouns that introduce this piece are not Hebrew names. The most likely location for them is in the Arabian peninsula. "Massa" was a name associated with the land of Ishmael (Gen. 25:14). It is very probable, however, that "Massa" as used here was not originally written as a proper noun but as a word for proverb, or oracle (see margin). In style and spirit verses 1-4 show some affinities with the oracles of Balaam in Numbers 22-24, which also have a non-Israelite setting.

The opening line of the oracle (vs. 1b) is even more mystifying than the title. The Hebrew text gives the impression that the names of persons are involved; the Revised Standard Version has tried to translate it accordingly but in the margin acknowledges the obscurity of the text. The Septuagint translators did not think the Hebrew text contained proper names; "these things says the man to those who trust in God and I cease" was their reading of it. Many modern interpreters think that the meaning has to do with the struggle to obtain wisdom, so that the opening line is an organic part of the paragraph.

The oracle proper ends with verse 4. In the Septuagint the first fourteen verses stand by themselves, showing that this was regarded as the limit of the piece; but, apart from that important precedent, it is hard to know why one should draw the line at verse 14. Unless one limits "the words of Agur" to the first paragraph (vss. 1-4), there is no good reason for not making them cover the entire chapter. However, to emphasize the distinction between the content and spirit of the first paragraph and what follows, the title will be treated as referring only to verses 1-4.

Agur confesses that he does not know wisdom; what is more, he does not know the one who does. With biting sarcasm he points out that others probably know the man who brought wisdom to earth; he does not! This is the word of a skeptic who doubts that man can ever discover the truth about his own existence; man cannot storm heaven and bring God down, he says. Only the Creator (vs. 4) could do that. Moreover, he does not acknowledge that God makes himself known by disclosing wisdom. We see at once that the viewpoint is radically different from that in which God's Wisdom comes to seek and invite men (1:20-33; 8:1-21; 9:1-6). It shares the view of Job 28 that man cannot discover God and his Wisdom; and it shares the dominant view of Ecclesiastes that God does not fully divulge his way to men.

Numerical Proverbs (30:5-33)

The gnomic patterns of every culture seem to include numerical devices as a way of accenting the points teachers want to make and of facilitating their memorization. This is also true in the case of Israel; prophets as well as sages made use of them (see Amos 1-2). This series is introduced by a stern reminder about the inexorable way and character of God (vss. 5-6); man cannot change God by adding to his words.

The "two things" asked for seem to be the absence of both falsehood and lying and poverty and riches; but only the latter pair is developed (vss. 7-9). The rich become too self-sufficient to remember God, and the poor too desperate to honor him. In verse 8c the passage anticipates the petition for "our daily bread" in the Lord's Prayer.

In verses 11-14 the numerical device is present in the fourfold repetition of "There are those." Lack of filial piety, self-righteousness, pride, and cruelty in word and act: these are the four ways of wickedness enumerated here.

Four examples of frustration are given in verses 15-16. Death, sterility, drought, and fire: these exhaust man's power and give him nothing in return.

Man can never fully rationally understand and explain the

phenomena of nature and the effect upon him of his involvement in them. The four examples of mystery in nature set forth in verses 18-19, chosen by a man in a pre-scientific society, do not wholly fail to arouse wonder even today.

Four examples of revolutionary chaos appear in verses 21-23. The sages were the enemies of social and political revolution, considering it a prime cause of oppression, violence, and disorder. These four illustrations all serve to underline their view.

Intelligence, reason, and order are more productive of good results than mere power (vss. 24-28). The sages apparently thought that even the animal world illustrates this principle. Here they offer four proofs; and as in most fables, in these illustrations the moral lesson is clear.

The Instruction of Lemuel (31:1-9)

This is a wholly independent piece in which a king's mother instructs her son in the ways of a strong and good rule. The fact that the instruction is offered by the mother is reminiscent of the fact that in the ancient Near East the mother of the king played a powerful role.

Lemuel is best thought of as a desert king, one of the "people of the east" in Arabia or Edom, regions famous for wisdom (I Kings 4:30; Jer. 49:7). The instruction emphasizes that a king's chief function is to rule in righteousness, and to be strong in the maintenance of the care of the poor (compare Ps. 72). To do so he must have a clear head: women (vs. 3) and wine (vs. 4) are the greatest threat to a good ruler. Women destroy the king's prowess as a warrior (Deut. 17:17). Wine dulls his mind in judgment; it is for the poor, to dull their pain, and for convicts at their execution. Jesus' refusal to take the wine offered him on the cross (Mark 15:23) is probably reported in order to draw attention to his kingship, especially on the cross, and to his judgment over sin and death.

An Acrostic on the Virtuous Wife (31:10-31)

Acrostic poems, in which each letter of the Hebrew alphabet is used in turn as the first letter of a line, are quite common in the Old Testament (Pss. 9-10, 25, 34, 37, 111, 112, 145; Lam. 1-4; Nahum 1:2-10). The most elaborate one is Psalm 119, in which each letter of the alphabet serves as the initial letter for eight successive lines.

The important role played by the wife despite her lack of legal rights is dealt with in chapter 18 (see comment). In this poem she is lauded for her virtues as a kind of home economist, and for her ingenuity as an industrious and farsighted manager. Initiative, strength, and aggressiveness mark her manner. She is a strong character with a well-clothed family. She "laughs at the time to come" (vs. 25) because she has all things so well in hand. Despite her engagement with life and affairs, she is wise, kind, and not forgetful of the poor. The blessings of her family (vs. 28) are her reward; she bestows "status" on her husband, so that he is a man apart even among the respected elders in the gate (vs. 23). She is a woman wholesome rather than feminine; all interest in "charm" or delicate refinements is foregone in favor of character and efficiency.

ECCLESIASTES

Historical Setting and Purpose

Ecclesiastes is the product of Israel's wisdom movement. Like the other canonical documents stemming from this movement, Job and Proverbs, it ignores the record of Israel's past, probably because its author, like the authors of Job and Proverbs, found no religious meaning in Israel's national history. In the Old Testament as a whole this history is read as the story of the saving activity of God, whether it begins with David, Moses, Abraham, or Adam. But a distinguishing feature of the wisdom movement, at least in its canonical period, is that it does not confess or make use of this heritage of historical revelation.

Since Ecclesiastes shows no interest in Israel's history and institutions, it contains no reference to external events or facts to facilitate locating it in Israel's past. There are references to the "king . . . in Jerusalem" (1:12), whom the title identifies as "son of David" (1:1). The author impersonates this king in 1:12—2:26 and clearly thinks of the era of the monarchy as a fabulous time of splendor and wealth (2:7-9). The era of Solomon was the era of splendor, and Solomon was the founder of the wisdom movement. Therefore, seeking to speak as profoundly as possible about the meaning of life, the author of this book says, in effect, "What would Solomon have said?" But this does not tell us who he was.

He is called "the Preacher" (1:1). We would probably have called him a critic or an essayist. The main role for such a man is to analyze an established view of life, probe its standard assertions, and expose the weaknesses and superficialities covered over by a repetition born of habit. This is precisely what this author does with the wisdom movement of his day as it is recorded for us in the Book of Proverbs. Although a representative of the wisdom movement himself, he breaks with its popular spokesmen. He accepts their method of examining the facts of

life to discover the truth about it, but he implies that their examination has not been thorough enough or that their conclusions
from it have lacked critical vigor. He concurs with them that
wisdom and folly differ as greatly as light and darkness (2:13),
but he disagrees about the significance of man's wisdom as a
means for one's knowledge of God. It is the purpose of the
writer not to condemn the empirical method of the sages but to
use it more thoroughly and face the findings without flinching.
All facts that bear upon man's situation must be taken into account, he insists. His very different evaluation of the possibilities
of man's life grow out of this more thorough and critical effort.
Like most critics, he is not so concerned to offer his own pre-
scriptions as he is to pick out the flaws in those in current use.

There can be little doubt that Ecclesiastes represents a reaction
to that stage of the wisdom movement represented by Proverbs.
It is therefore proper to consider it a later document, probably
even later than the youngest part of Proverbs. The fourth or third
century of the pre-Christian era would be the most likely time for
it. This coincides with the end of the era of the Persian empire
and the coming of the Greeks. In this connection it may be
noted that the word "parks" (2:5) is a Persian word identical
with our word "paradise." It has long been debated whether
Greek influences may also be discerned. The demonstration of
these might result in assigning a later date to the book. While it
cannot be said that this matter is settled, it does seem fair to
say that there is a growing rejection of the idea of any Greek
influence. This is due mostly to the fact that those ideas in the
book once thought to be of Greek origin have also been found
in the cultural legacy of the ancient Near East, rediscovered by
archaeology. A more satisfactory understanding of the setting
of Ecclesiastes and its purpose is achieved by reading it as a
criticism of some of the themes in Proverbs, and as a special facet
in the history of Israel's wisdom movement, than by attempting
to fit it into a chronology of external events.

Koheleth, to use "the Preacher's" Hebrew title, works with the
same empirical methods as the earlier sages. It is his purpose to
show that the generalizations they made on the basis of their
findings are both too sweeping and too absolute in character.
Thus, for example, as Proverbs shows us, the sages insisted that
the "wise" or "righteous" would always be prosperous, respected,
and wealthy. The "foolish" and "wicked" would be the very

opposite. Koheleth shows that the actual evidence from real life does not support this teaching. Moreover, the sages taught that the wisdom about life they discovered and accumulated gave them a sure clue to the goal of man's life; that is, that it constituted an insight into the ways of God, especially as these had a bearing upon man's destiny. Thus wisdom was given the status of an absolute good. But Koheleth argues persistently and convincingly that this is not so. He agrees that man's understanding of his world and of himself—"education" would be our word for it—is, indeed, a great and important good. But it is only a relative good, a "better." By implication he says that those who treat it as an absolute good, as the way by which God is found and understood, make an idol of wisdom. His repeated admonition to enjoy life and its possibilities and comforts day by day (2:24-26; 3:12-13, 22; 5:18-20) must not be taken as a recipe for irresponsible self-indulgence but as a corollary of the rejection of the idea that man can hold his future in his own hand (see 9:11). In the last analysis, however important its relative value, all man's wisdom and action is "vanity": that is, it does not serve to penetrate the mystery that shrouds the ways of God; and, since God is the real arbiter of the meaning of all life, it does not really clarify the meaning of the human situation. Koheleth's favorite way of arguing this vanity or relativity of all man's aims, knowledge, and plans is to point to the inescapable fact of death. In contrast to Proverbs, the fact of death becomes a central issue in this book (1:11; 2:12-16; 3:19-21; 5:15-16; 6:6; 7:2; 9:1-6, 12; 12:1-7). Death illustrates the transiency and vanity of all. Man must never overlook these characteristics of his own life, therefore it is better to go to a wake than to a feast (7:2). To sum up the purpose: Koheleth seeks to puncture the pretensions of the wisdom movement about the meaning of the truth man can discover; he wants to show that the gap that separates man from God is infinitely wider than writers of a book such as Proverbs seem to imply.

The Literary Form of Ecclesiastes

How did this critic go about his work? It is clear that he was a literary craftsman, an essayist. One of his editors (12:9) says that he weighed, studied, and arranged proverbs "with great care," which sums up the matter very well. As he pondered the questions that troubled him, he worked over the received collections of proverbs and no doubt simply quoted a good number of these to make his points (for example, 1:15 or 8:5). He also took such proverbs and changed them to make them give his own special insight (7:13). In many cases it is simply impossible to decide whether an item is a quote or a fresh coinage (for example, 11:9), but in the case of sayings such as 1:18 the substance argues firmly for originality.

But Koheleth was not just an editor of proverbs, or an imitative composer. As an essayist he is versatile and ingenious. It is remarkable what a large variety of stylistic forms he was able to utilize. There is, for example, his very frequent use of the rhetorical question, either as a means of getting across an implied point or to introduce a little essay (1:3, 10; 3:9, 22; 5:6, 11, 16-17; 6:8, 12; 8:1). And there is the unforgettable poem built up around the rhythmic word (3:2-8). In 10:16-17 there is an example of a "Woe," a form popular in prophetic writing, and of a "Beatitude," more characteristic of the sages, set in fine parallel. The numerical device (see Prov. 30) is not so clearly in evidence, but the sayings in 3:15 and 8:8 are probably under its influence. The admonition in the imperative, a commandment form, occurs quite frequently (for example, 11:1, 2), and there is at least one instance of the conditional form (6:3), also associated with the legal tradition (Exod. 21-23). An example of allegory is found in 12:3-5.

In addition to this skillful utilization of a very wide selection of current forms there are three additional ones which make it possible to claim for Koheleth a really remarkable degree of originality:

1. He makes very frequent use of the first person to present his convictions as a matter of personal experience or discovery: "I said to myself" or "I said in my heart" (1:16; 2:1, 15; 3:17, 18; also "I say," 6:3; see comment on 9:16), "I found" (7:26, 27), "I know" (3:12, 14), and "I have seen" or "I saw" or "I perceived" (1:14, 17; 2:14; 3:10, 16, 22; 4:1, 4, 7, 15; 5:13, 18; 6:1; 7:15; 8:10, 17; 9:11, 13).

2. The personal relation or confession is often illustrated by means of what we may call a "story" or a "picture" (for example, 5:13-15; 6:2-3; 9:14-15).

3. Perhaps most distinctive of all, there is the "better" saying. There are six examples of this in 7:1-12 and several more in

various places (2:24; 3:12, 22; 4:6, 9, 13; 5:5; 9:16-18). What is striking about these is that the form corresponds to the idea; Koheleth's relativism makes use of the comparative adjective (see comment on 7:1-12).

All three of these forms developed in such an original way by Koheleth live on in the sayings of Jesus in the Gospels.

Ecclesiastes and the Biblical Message

It has already been noted that it was Koheleth's purpose to correct the sages who thought that by piety and wisdom men could discover God. For him God remains inscrutable. God has made everything (3:11) and has implanted in man's heart the desire to know him; but man cannot attain this knowledge by an analysis of the world God has made. Unlike Proverbs, Ecclesiastes puts little confidence in what we call "natural revelation." As a good sage, Koheleth does not begin with a confession of God that appeals to a special revelation such as is represented by the call of Abraham or the Exodus and the Covenant at Sinai. Thus for him God remains hidden, the "Wholly Other"; man can build no bridges to him.

This author does believe that God has "a time" for everything; that is, that in its own way each process, event, and person fits into the plan of God. But man does not know what this plan is or how a given aspect of life functions in it. The "time" of a thing is always out of order from man's point of view (9:11-12). That God makes even the wrath of men praise him Koheleth would readily have accepted, thus differing with Proverbs; but it would have troubled him (8:6).

Koheleth not only acknowledges God as universal ruler who utilizes all; he confesses his goodness. Therefore, even though he cannot know the nature of this goodness or what God will make of everything, he can relax and enjoy life. In his enjoyment of the material and sensate possibilities of life (4:7-11) he is a real Israelite; and his admonitions to eat, drink, and have pleasure usually come at points in his essay when he has established the impossibility that man can discover God. We cannot know God, he says; but we know his world is a gift to be enjoyed. Koheleth recovers a theocentric view of life that Proverbs and the wisdom movement generally tended to qualify. Moreover, he has made a break with the sort of legalism that makes the achievement of human destiny a goal for man to attain. He is set free from the Law in a very different way from the Apostle Paul, but set free none the less. The radical monotheism of Koheleth could lead to a passive resignation or even to cynicism; but, thanks to his abiding confidence that he lived in a good world that God had given him to enjoy, this did not happen in his case.

Ecclesiastes is one of the developments in the later period of the Old Testament that set the stage for the New. For the New Testament builds upon the view of Koheleth that God alone knows what man needs; and it combines this with the general view of the Bible that he discloses this not through a human search and discovery but by special historical events which are the acts of his redeeming grace.

OUTLINE

The Title (1:1)
The Preacher's Theme (1:2)
The Net Profit of Man's Living (1:3-11)
Wisdom Versus Folly (1:12—2:26)
Knowledge of the "Times" and Their Mystery (3:1-15)
Two Examples of Injustice (3:16—4:3)
The Doctrine of Work: Two Criticisms (4:4-12)
The Self-Made Man (4:13-16)
Man Before God (5:1-7)
Political Corruption (5:8-9)
The Possibilities and Problems of Property (5:10—6:12)
What Gives Security? (7:1-14)
The Relativity of Righteousness (7:15-22)
Female Deviousness (7:23-29)
The Ruler (8:1-8)
Man's Inhumanity to Man (8:9-15)
God's Work and Man's Quest (8:16—9:12)
Wisdom Slighted (9:13—10:3)
Assorted Sayings (10:4-20)
Life as Risk and Possibility (11:1-8)
Youth and Age (11:9—12:7)
Conclusion: The Theme (12:8)
Two Postscripts (12:9-14)

COMMENTARY

The Title (1:1)

The title draws on 1:12 in its assertion that the author of this book was "king in Jerusalem." But it wants to make the point that he was Solomon; so it introduces the words "son of David." Solomon was the founder and patron of Israel's wisdom movement (see the Introduction to Proverbs). This title makes the point that Ecclesiastes is a product of this movement and that its author was a sage. This is also indicated by the phrase "The words of the Preacher" (compare Prov. 30:1; 31:1). In 12:10, part of an editorial conclusion for this book, we are told that the Preacher sought to find "words of truth" and that he wrote them down. In the Book of Proverbs the sayings of the sages are commonly described as "words." The suggestion that the editor who added 12:9-10 also provided this title seems in order.

The author of the book had described himself as "Preacher"— Koheleth (1:2, 12; 7:27; 12:8), and the editor who composed this title used the same term. It is derived from the Hebrew verb "to assemble," from which a word for "congregation" is also derived. Koheleth is the man who assembles the congregation to address them as a "preacher." The word "Ecclesiastes" comes from a Greek verb meaning "to hold an assembly" and refers to a member or convener of such an assembly.

The Preacher's Theme (1:2)

This verse may stand by itself, or it may be thought of as being organically of a piece with verses 3-11. In either case it states the theme for the entire book, not only for 1:3-11. Its substance is repeated in abbreviated form in 12:8, which probably marks the end of the book proper, the remainder consisting of a series of editorial conclusions. This verse plays a role in Ecclesiastes similar to the role of Proverbs 1:7 in that book.

The word "vanity" connotes the opposite of substantial. It refers to the evanescent and transitory in contrast to the permanent. The Hebrew word from which it comes has the basic meaning of the transiency of the breath one can "see" on a cold morning. "All is vanity," says the Preacher. What he means is that nothing in life, nor all of it together, "adds up to anything." One's work, learning, and pleasure yield no permanent results. The key to the significance of life is not in man's possession; therefore he cannot attain the true goal of his life as the sages in Proverbs had said he could. So man's life is "vain" (6:12; 7:15; 9:9), bereft of a real goal and an attainable destiny. We read in the Old Testament about the "heaven of heavens" (Deut. 10:14; I Kings 8:27), to designate the farthest reaches; about "the Song of Songs" (Song of Solomon 1:1), to designate the perfect song. So here and in 12:8 the author speaks about life's meaninglessness as a "vanity of vanities," to emphasize its ultimate and devastating implications. What he confesses is that, in the last analysis, when all is said and done, man cannot save himself.

The Net Profit of Man's Living (1:3-11)

Since 1:12 contains a part of the title in 1:1 it has often been held that it was once the opening sentence of the book and that the poem in verses 3-11 was introduced later, possibly by the editor who devised the title in 1:1. If this be indeed the case, the editor deserves great credit for having selected or composed a poetic essay that in a profound and comprehensive way sums up the problem dealt with in Ecclesiastes throughout: namely, the meaning of a man's life.

The poem cites the repetitive character of many of nature's processes: the coming and going of generations, sunrise and sunset, the turning of the wind, and the flowing of the streams that never can fill the sea. As a result the poem has sometimes been dealt with as though it were a little essay in cosmic philosophy which seeks to propound a thesis of universal determinism. But this is misleading; and it imputes to the Old Testament and its environment a theoretical and systematic philosophical interest and method shared by the modern West with ancient Greece, but alien to Israel and its Semitic neighbors. Besides, it overlooks the title line of the poem.

Coming out of the wisdom movement, the poem is interested in man. What can man achieve, and by what means? Can he really, by the discipline of wisdom, come to see the true end of his life, as Proverbs teaches, and, in his own disciplined living, move toward it? That is the question raised in verse 3a. The word for "gain," used in no other Old Testament book, is a noun drawn from the world of business; it refers to profit, a return on an investment. The poem asks whether there is any net result to man's struggle to see and attain his meaning and end. The sages taught that man must participate fully and actively in life. Ecclesiastes assumes that one does this, and it is not oblivious to the advantage (2:13) of such participation. The sage can learn much and enrich his life in many ways and find satisfaction and enjoyment in the process. But does what he discovers and enjoys contribute to his progress to his ultimate goal? The Preacher has decided that it does not, thus breaking with the sages who wrote Proverbs. His conclusion relativizes his life and its meaning in every respect. His search for meaning and understanding, while practically useful, is no longer of ultimate significance; it does not determine or define his final destiny. For the Preacher, who had been taught that learning could be an avenue to the knowledge of God's way with man, this is depressing and destroys his zest for living.

This relativization of the meaning of all man's experience and effort, and the ensuing tendency to listlessness, is the subject of verse 8, which answers the question raised in verse 3. In the translation of 8a in the Revised Standard Version the term "things" serves as a synonym for all the repetitive natural phenomena cited in verses 4-7. But, apart from the fact that the Preacher is not that much of a philosopher, this is a very dubious translation of the Hebrew for 8a, especially in view of 8b. The word for "things" also means "words," which is what it probably means here. There is no Hebrew basis for either "full" or "it," and "weariness" is an adjective rather than a noun. The line might be better translated as follows: "All words are weak; a man is not able to speak." That is, even the sage cannot put the meaning of life into words. The Book of Proverbs taught that if one turned one's ear to the sages to hear their words and if one used one's eyes to advantage in studying his human and natural environment, one would become wise; that is, he would be able to speak with explicit finality about the meaning of life and about the way to attain it. This the Preacher disputes.

In Proverbs, maturity and old age are viewed with great respect because they are synonymous with lasting achievement. Life is long enough, because its meaning can be attained. But for Ecclesiastes it is never long enough, because its meaning is unattainable. The recital of the repetitiveness in nature (vss. 4-7) and of the lack of novelty in its processes (vss. 9-11) serves the author in two ways: it draws attention to his own experience of a life made too brief by its meaninglessness; and, since the repetitive natural processes produce nothing new, it confirms his conviction that he will not discover life's meaning. It is simply not possible to do so. The unchanging constancies of nature serve the author to illustrate his view of the human situation.

The most striking thing about the viewpoint displayed here is that it remains strictly focused on man. It avoids a theological as well as a philosophical alternative. In nearly every part of the Bible, including Proverbs 1-9, the doctrine of man is an inference from faith's confession about the character and work of God. The constancies of nature are broken by the acts of God, which, for faith, produce a "new thing" (Isa. 43:19; see also Num. 16:30); and the dynamic actuality of the living God outlasts the endurance of the world it called into being (Ps. 102:25-27). But Koheleth rarely employs these themes of historical revelation or of creation in his thinking. He goes further than Proverbs in this, for he not only avoids the particular events of Israel's faith but also ignores the notion of the latest section of Proverbs that God is seeking to disclose himself to man. Thus the constancy of nature cannot remind him of the faithfulness of God, but only of his own weakness and transiency. However, it is out of this experience of man's helplessness and finitude that Koheleth begins to move again toward a God-centered point of view about life, even though it remains largely implicit; that is, God for him becomes decisive again, but remains unknown.

Wisdom Versus Folly (1:12—2:26)

In this discourse Koheleth describes some of the concrete attempts he made to find a basis for purposeful living. His statement "I . . . have been king" (1:12) may be interpreted to mean that he is in imagination playing the role of Solomon at the end of his life and asking about its meaning. He makes his search for a purpose for life as a sage, "by wisdom" (1:13). This search is one that is unavoidable; it is an inescapable fact of one's humanity, an obligation God puts upon one. A man who neglects it is a fool. Nevertheless, for the man who undertakes it, the obligation proves to be "an unhappy business" (1:13), a cause of frustration. A man is called to wisdom; but when he heeds this call and attempts to state the difference between wisdom and folly (1:17) he is confronted by the fact that the ultimate fate of wise and fools is the same (2:15). Therefore, there is no decisive significance to his contrast between wisdom and folly, and the attempt to make it is "a striving after wind" (2:17). For Koheleth, the difference between the wise man and the fool has become a relative thing. He quotes two proverbs (1:15, 18) to make his point: one can analyze the facts, but one cannot change them; and when a wise man discovers that his knowledge cannot alter his fate, his "sorrow" has increased proportionately. The fool does not know the truth, but he also escapes its burden.

In 2:1-11 Koheleth reports how, in his effort to find an abiding purpose in life, he worked with the possibility that one might discover the key to it by throwing one's self completely into the sensate activities of life. In imagination he relived the career of Solomon (see I Kings 5-11). He became a builder of palaces and gardens, the monarch of an oriental court replete with "wine, women, and song." Although a sage, he does not think about life as would a schoolman in an ivory tower but as the man of action, fully engaged, giving direction to the ferment of social and material existence all around him. He made "great works" (2:4) so that he surpassed all who had preceded him (2:9). We note the motives of competition and of self-realization through one's accomplishments. Might these carry in them or give a clue to the significance of a man's life? He also looked for the answer by gratifying without restraint his desires for personal satisfaction. In both cases (2:3, 9) his wisdom guided him; that is, he threw himself into these affairs to see how they might answer his questions about the real meaning and purpose of life. Unlike many moderns who pursue a very similar course of life, he does raise the issue of the ultimate meaning of his "toil" and satisfactions. But he seems to end up with precisely the same conclusions about which modern man often speaks: namely, that while this career of competition, action, accomplishment, and indulgence offers no clue to an ultimate meaning, it is rewarding for its own sake; the struggle and excitement itself "was my reward for all my toil" (2:10). The game as such is the thing, he says; you play it because you enjoy it, for its own sake, not for any purpose or meaning to which it points. This point is made even more explicitly in 2:24, and it becomes a steady and recurrent theme of the book. This is, of course, a very common modern theme ("Business is my game; I play it because I enjoy it, and for me it is enough"). For Koheleth, however, it did not provide the answer he sought (2:11). By throwing himself into the world of human action he found only relative purposes and values, no ultimate meaning or goal.

The paragraph consisting of 2:12-17 makes the point that the superiority of wisdom over folly is very great in a practical and relative sense, but that ultimately it makes no difference; neither a man's knowledge nor his capacities for self-discipline and constructive accomplishment count in the end.

It is best, perhaps, to consider verse 12b as a comment inserted into the argument by a scribe or interpreter who wanted to press the actual history of Solomon as the inspiration for the comparison. Rehoboam was foolish (I Kings 12); but, after all, as successor to the great and wise Solomon, what could he have done that had not already been done? But these sentences really stand outside of the progress of thought in the paragraph.

The relative superiority of wisdom, as great as the difference between day and night, is illustrated by an antithetical proverb (vs. 14): "The wise man has his eyes in his head . . ." But since a wise man who senses the implications of his situation as a man can do nothing about them, his very advantage becomes a source of anxiety; he is troubled and worried the way a fool or ignorant man never is. What his wisdom helps him to see is that the same "fate" (vs. 14), the same encounter, that awaits the fool awaits him also; that is, the encounter with death. For this man the bitterness of death consists in the fact that it ultimately ends in the complete extinction of one's memory; eventually no one will know he ever existed. For the most part, Israel confessed no faith in individual resurrection (but see Daniel 12). What comforted the individual confronted by death was his membership in a community, in Israel. His "name," the reality of what he was in his being and in his deeds, would live on in the community as a whole, beginning with his own descendants. The raising of monuments and memorials, which seems to have increased in later centuries, must be seen in part as an attempt to illustrate this confidence and in part as a substitute for it. Koheleth, like most of the sages, is too much of an individualist to derive much comfort from this Israelite notion of a "social immortality" that rests on the Covenant of Israel with God. And he is too wise not to know that even the most enduring material sign erected to his life and work will eventually crumble or be forgotten. Man has "no enduring remembrance" (vs. 16); therefore even the life of the sage is at bottom without meaning.

Having established the transient character of his own life, the sage (2:18-23) is doubly convinced about the meaninglessness of all his works: they cannot alter his own fate; and when they fall into the hands of those who come after, and who can never appreciate the intentions of their founder, they will mock all the effort he put into them. So the "strain" and "toil" of life are meaningless; the sage's analysis has undercut the motivation for industry as well as for wisdom.

What is left? To enjoy *now* that which offers itself for man's enjoyment (2:24-26). Koheleth has reached the conclusion that since all values are impermanent and relative, long-range goals are always disillusioning. Immediately available satisfactions, however transient, are to be accepted as gifts of God. The fact that even these are available to some and not to others further complicates the riddle of life and illustrates its basic meaninglessness. Koheleth evaluates life from the viewpoint of human possibility—as Proverbs had done—and he finds it meaningless. By stressing man's impotence he is, indirectly, preparing the wisdom movement for a basic reorientation in the direction of a God-centered faith.

Knowledge of the "Times" and Their Mystery (3:1-15)

The writers of Proverbs exulted in what we would call "the freedom of man." They were impressed by man's ability to make natural and social processes serve his purposes. To be sure, this demanded intense training and a regimen of self-discipline. But they held that if a man would meet the conditions, he could attain the goals of his life, and the processes of the world would be his allies. This, of course, corresponds rather closely to the optimistic outlook of religious and democratic liberalism prevalent at the opening of this century, notably in the new world of America. Whereas for Proverbs rational intelligence and the formation of character through self-discipline were the means to the end, the modern means were seen mainly in the applications of scientific method to bring about technological and social transformations.

The mood of western man today differs from that prevalent at the beginning of the century mainly because men have lost confidence in their ability to make nature—space, time, and matter—serve their purposes in an ultimately significant way. They do not experience nature as the bearer of a revelation about man's life understandable to man. This very different mood corresponds in many ways to the change in mood that distinguishes Koheleth from Proverbs. This is illustrated by 3:1-15.

This author is not interested in time, represented by the endless ticking of a clock; he is interested in "a time" or in "times," moments of happening, time as a series of turning points or events. In Proverbs such moments tended to become a human option, the appropriate matching of a human word or action with a situation (see, for example, Prov. 15:23), thus illustrating human freedom. But in the Bible as a whole they were seen rather as aspects of the operation of the purpose of God. They were shrouded in mystery and evoked dread. The prophets were interpreters of the "times" in this context, disclosing the ways of God to man. Wise men, too, were sometimes thought to know the "times" of God (Esther 1:13). But God remained in charge of the "times," whether the turning points of history as a whole or of an individual human life. Man "received" his "times" from God (Ps. 31:15; Rom. 14:8). Included in such "receiving" was a disclosure of God's use of them in his purpose for man. This made the "times" not only bearable; they became also anticipated moments of joy and exultation.

Unlike Proverbs, Koheleth does not incline to the notion that man creates his own "times"; this is well illustrated in 3:2a by the "time" that leads off the series. A man has nothing to say about being born, and little or nothing about dying. Koheleth acknowledges that the moments in human life come from God. He is even ready to admit that God has made "everything beautiful in its time" (3:11), a statement probably reflecting his knowledge of the story of Creation (see Gen. 1:4, 12, 18, 21, 25, 31). But the "times" conceived as signs of the action of God bring him no joy. The mystery remains a riddle. God has made man with the desire to know the meaning of the events that befall him, he "has put eternity into man's mind" (3:11), but man cannot fulfill this desire because his contemplation of the "times" does not make him see what God has done "from the beginning to the end"; that is, that all things work together for the realiza-

tion of man's true end. What God does endures forever. But
since man cannot give an account of the mystery on this grand
scale, he must resign himself to enjoying the immediate and
relative satisfactions life has to offer: his food, his drink, and his
work in terms of what they are as such rather than in terms of
what they point to or help to bring about.

Two Examples of Injustice (3:16—4:3)

Up to now Koheleth has been busy with questions of a philosophical sort: the meaning of human existence, man's freedom
or lack of it, and so on. But now he turns to strictly ethical
examples of irrationality that mock man's search for a good and
meaningful life. He questions the teaching of Proverbs that the
difference between righteousness and evil, as man describes it,
marks the line that determines man's destiny.

The first example (3:16-22) relates to the courts. If there is
one thing on which all spokesmen in Israel can agree—sages
and psalmists, prophets and scribes—it is that the community's
legal processes must be pure. Bribery, false testimony, and con-
nivance are abhorred (Ps. 15); justice must be blindfolded, for
the Lord himself is not a respecter of persons. It is firmly believed that the permanence of the community and the happiness
of the individual are assured by the observance of the moral and
legal sanctities. But Koheleth has seen that these are never truly
kept: in the very place where righteousness should be vindicated,
"even there was wickedness" (vs. 16). He considers the sages of
Proverbs too sanguine, even naïve; there is no simple pattern of
black and white in life. All is gray in the realm of moral action.
It becomes impossible for any man to distinguish clearly between
the righteous and the wicked; he is left without a clear norm by
which to live.

Thus, even morally and ethically man-centered life becomes
frustrating and vain. Koheleth does not doubt (vs. 17) that God
will separate the wheat from the tares (see Matt. 13:24-30, 36-
43), for he is the Judge of all and provides a "time" for all at
which life's real meaning will be tallied. But this outcome lies in
the future, and man is not privy to the criteria that establish it.

Why does God keep people in the dark in this way, asks
Koheleth. He provides an answer in verses 18-22. It is to remind
men of their creaturehood; they are "men, and not God" (Isa.

31:3). Indeed, reacting against the tendency of Proverbs to exalt the power of man and make him equal to God in respect to his knowledge of the ways of God, Koheleth wonders whether man is much more than a beast (vs. 18). Really, says Koheleth, all men are fools ("beasts") when their knowledge is set over against God's, even the wise. Thus he pricks the pretense of the sages.

He illustrates his point about the affinity between man and beast by reminding his readers that both die; "as one dies, so dies the other" (vs. 19). In elaborating this idea he offers an interpretation of the account of Creation in Genesis 2-3; that is, all have the same breath and "all turn to dust" (vs. 20; Gen. 2:7, 19; 3:19). God formed both man and beast out of the ground and made both to be living creatures. But only about man does Genesis say that God breathed into his nostrils. Some of Koheleth's contemporaries apparently used this as proof of their belief that at death only the life or spirit of man returned to God. Koheleth did not deny that life returned to God (12:7). But was this true only of human life? "Who knows . . . ?" he says. The point he really wishes to make is that the fact that man's breath of life was a gift of God was no guarantee that man shared the understanding of God, as was commonly held (see Job 32:8; 33:4). The difference between a wise man and a fool is only relative, not absolute. Since also in terms of moral distinctions it is impossible for man to know God's "time" in moral judgment, Koheleth repeats his advice to man to enjoy what is given him in his own day (vs. 22; compare 2:24-26; 3:12-13; John 7:6).

Koheleth now offers a second example (4:1-3) from practical life to show that it is impossible to prove the power and goodness of God by means of an analysis of the ethical dimensions of social process. This example illustrates the demonic character of power in the hands of men, and the helplessness of its victims. Koheleth finds superficial the generalization of Proverbs that the wise and the good will be powerful. He has become a "realist." Power feeds on power; a structure must employ force to maintain itself. Koheleth has discovered a bitter "law" about social and economic power which had won the status of an axiom in the days of Jesus (Matt. 13:12): power is difficult to control, and the weak are comfortless. This was true even in Israel, with its suspicion of power and its prophetic injunction to comfort the fatherless and the widow.

When Koheleth contemplated this situation he concluded that the lot of the dead was better than that of the living. He has a penchant for relative comparisons (see 2:13), rather than for the favored antithesis of Proverbs, and develops a proverbial form based on the comparative principle of "yes—but" (see 7:1-12). Here, however, he introduces a third and even more preferable option—never to have been (compare Job 3:1-19; Jer. 20:14-18). In thus piling a comparison upon a comparison he stresses the hopelessness of man's quest for meaning in an examination of the ethical dimensions of his social existence. It is instructive to note, however, that Koheleth does not curse the day of his birth, as did Job and Jeremiah; he makes comparisons!

The Doctrine of Work: Two Criticisms (4:4-12)

In Proverbs (see the comment on chs. 12 and 26) industrious-ness is treated as a virtue and idleness as a vice. The contrast is virtually absolute. The impression is created that a man can justify his life in terms of hard work. It is assumed that the motives of the hardworking man are of the best and that his efforts will result in a demonstration of the moral goodness and sovereignty of God. Here Koheleth offers two criticisms of this outlook.

In the first (4:4-6) he raises the issue of motive. Men do not work for idealistic reasons, he says; "all" their toil and skill spring from a competitive desire to win. Industry becomes a mark of jealousy; work separates a man from his neighbor. Far from becoming a means of self-realization, it becomes an obsession. Industriousness is not a pure testimony to the goodness of life; it can be a reminder of its venom.

At this point the author is reminded of the lazy fool with folded hands the sages talk about (Prov. 6:10; 24:33). Surely the improvident man who "eats his own flesh" is an example to be avoided at all costs. This brings him into a typical "yes—but" state of mind which evokes a saying beginning with the charac-teristic "better": "Better is a handful of quietness than two hands full of toil" for Koheleth because of the questionable significance of all human action.

In the second example, as in the first, Koheleth begins with a personal observation. There is a man who literally lives only to work. Work can produce wealth, and he is hungry for wealth.

Wealth has become an end in itself for this man. Some work out of envy; this man because of avarice. He has "no one"; this lack of heirs or companions simply underscores the point also made in the first example, that work can destroy one's humanity rather than be the means of its realization as the sages taught. Taken in this way, it is not a basis on which to build one's life.

In verses 9-12 Koheleth ponders the advantages of human companionship and mutual assistance. The little essay reads like a series of proverbs interspersed with Koheleth's words, to present his thought. The connection with the problem stated in verses 7-8 is not direct; verse 9b is a somewhat clumsy way of alluding to it. What he seems to intimate is that, relatively speaking, human community and mutuality form a more promising basis for the significance of life than does work.

The Self-Made Man (4:13-16)

The sages had great respect for the office and person of the ruler (see Prov. 20). The very thought of the displacement of a king by an unworthy person was abhorrent (Prov. 19:10). But it was also recognized that a king could demean the dignity of his office (Prov. 17:7), forfeit his privilege. Moreover, the theme of the poor but honest boy, devoted to wisdom and work, who became wealthy and respected was a popular one. In this paragraph Koheleth begins with this motif. Yes, the poor, wise boy does have an advantage over the old, foolish king. He is "better." Koheleth draws a dramatic picture: in his own realm, where he had been born poor and had been in prison, the "youth" rises to the top. In imagination Koheleth is one of the massive crowd that hails the virtuous youth who comes to displace the old king. (In verse 15, margin, he is designated as "second," perhaps an allusion to the story of Joseph's use of power in Genesis 41:43.) But the time will come when this ideal youth will also have had his day. This great achievement, however praiseworthy and heartening, is also transient. The sages had taught that there was a continuous path from this sort of accomplishment to the attainment of man's final destiny. Koheleth denies this. The finest and noblest achievements of men are the works of creatures: they pass away. He does not speak about the fickleness of the crowd or of the inconstancy of the young ruler; the matter is more subtle. He is sad rather than cynical. The best that man can achieve must always be evaluated with a "yes—but." Koheleth has undercut the man-based optimism of the sages.

Man Before God (5:1-7)

Here, in four separate sayings, the Preacher speaks about man's proper deportment in the presence of God, although, like the sages of Proverbs, he seldom speaks of matters of religious practice. These sayings seem to show that his experience of man's situation has also influenced his thought in respect to what is proper in worship.

The first saying (5:1) states that one must approach God "to listen." In general the sages deprecated sacrifices. Obedience to the will of God was much more important (see Prov. 21). The prophets counted love of God, with obedience, as superior to sacrifice (Hosea 6:6). Koheleth gives the preference to hearing or listening. This could be construed as a listening to the explanations of the will of God by the sages, as in Proverbs. But it seems more appropriate to contrast it with speaking (compare James 1:19). The proper attitude of man before God is reverent silence. He is before the impenetrable mystery which, though it remains a mystery, he must ponder because it determines his destiny.

The second saying (5:2-3) also assumes the gulf between God and man. This distance would make the multiplication of words meaningless for Koheleth; in the New Testament the care of God makes them unnecessary (Matt. 6:8). In any event, both assume a centrality for the role of God which must be taken seriously in our thought about prayer.

In the third saying (5:4-5) Koheleth repeats the substance of the law of the vow (Deut. 23:22-24). A vow is a voluntary matter. No blame attaches to not taking a vow; but, once made, it must be fulfilled. Koheleth's despair about revelation does not relativize his conviction about the binding character of a religious act.

As in the case of sacrifice, prayer, and vow, so also in respect to one's relation with God through the priest, "the messenger" (vs. 6; see Mal. 2:7), restraint and modesty are the expression of the fear of God. Sins of inadvertence could be atoned for (Num. 15:22-31). But can irresponsible talk be so easily dismissed? Why jeopardize one's whole life? Awe or reverence expressed in silence exemplifies what Koheleth means by fear of God.

Political Corruption (5:8-9)

Koheleth returns once again (see 3:16—4:3) to the phenomenon of legal corruption and oppression. He does not bemoan it but seems to concede its inevitability. He simply tells his readers not to be amazed. He draws a picture of a bureaucratic hierarchy whose very structure and function seem to assume injustice and corruption: there are watchers and those who watch the watchers. The sages were ardent royalists (see the comment on Prov. 20) who exalted the king as the symbol of justice and civic virtue. Although he no longer shares their idealism Koheleth acknowledges that, at least in a settled land, rule by a king is perhaps the best sort of government.

The Possibilities and Problems of Property (5:10—6:12)

In this section Koheleth makes a series of observations on man's struggle to obtain possessions. He notes that wealth is a source of inequity and that, even for those who obtain it, it is a mixed blessing. As always, his purpose is to demonstrate that this aspect of human experience also shows that man has no proof of the significance of his life: it is vanity.

In verse 10 the author offers a comment on what was probably a common saying: the desire for money and gain is insatiable. But this does not lead him to moralize about greed; he seems to assume that it is inevitable, or at least that it is an illustration of the inconclusiveness of man's life. Man is always reaching for a goal he never attains; this is the riddle of the human situation, says Koheleth. The search for wealth is one more example of it; it also points up the meaninglessness of life.

In verse 11 Koheleth points out that a man whose property increases is beset by many hangers-on who use it up. He is attacking the teaching of the sages (see Prov. 19) that wealth constitutes a substantial good. The note of wry humor present here continues in verse 12: a laborer can sleep. There is no intention to exalt the laborer's state, but to stress once more the ambiguous nature of wealth.

Property does not necessarily ensure the perpetuation of a family line; in any case its individual possessor is separated from it by death. This, in summary, is the meaning of verses 13-17. The unit consists of two parts, as the word "also" in 16a, which repeats 13a, shows; but there is a continuity in the thought. The real subject is the very relative significance of property; but so great is the almost morbid fascination of death for Koheleth that, though he only wanted to use it as an illustration, it almost displaces the issue under discussion.

As he frequently does, Koheleth presents the issue in the form of a case he had himself observed: a man had wealth which he lost in a "bad venture," presumably an unwise investment. We can only guess why he had held this wealth "to his hurt" (vs. 13). Koheleth may mean that, inasmuch as the riches were lost anyway, it would have been much better if they had been used for everyday enjoyment; certainly, they served no great goals. The man has a son who will perpetuate his memory; but since there is no legacy for him, the wealth he once toiled for contributes nothing to the memory to be perpetuated by the son. The man is at the end of his life; he will go "naked as he came" (vs. 15; see Job 1:21). That a man cannot as an individual take his wealth with him at death is obvious. We must connect verse 15 with the point made in verse 14 that there is nothing for the son who perpetuates the man's name; the man is "naked" in his grave because, despite the fact that he had a son, there is no witness to his accomplishment on earth, no lands or buildings to point to. It is a pity, says the author, that such a man ever treated wealth as though it were a self-transcending medium. He "toiled for the wind" and spent his "days in darkness" (see Ps. 90:10) precisely because he entertained long-range hopes. He should not have been "anxious about tomorrow" (Matt. 6:34), but should have let every day take care of itself.

What might have been for this man whose case has just been analyzed is expressed in the next paragraph (vss. 18-20). Wealth and possessions are of no ultimate significance, says Koheleth; they neither disclose nor help man to attain a divinely appointed destiny. God does not give them for that (vs. 19), but for the sweetening of life day by day. The brevity and burden of life will not be much remembered by a man who uses his money as God intends. "God keeps him occupied with joy in his heart"; that is, with the eating and drinking made possible by the results of man's work. For Koheleth the burden of responsibility (or of the Law), so intense in Proverbs, has disappeared. All human values are relativized because none of them is the means to man's true end. In this respect he anticipates the view of Paul; what he lacks is the latter's clarity and conviction about this

end and about the love and power of God by which it is given.
Hence, with his relativizing of all human undertakings there
comes a serious loss of purpose and commitment.

In 6:1-6 Koheleth presents another example in support of his
thesis that wealth is no guarantee of security. In 5:13-17 he dis-
cussed the possibility of losing possessions. Here he emphasizes
the point that a man may be deprived of their enjoyment even
when they are not lost, whether because of illness or for some
other reason. Formally speaking, such a man's position is impressive: "wealth, posessions, and honor" (vs. 2) belong to
him, but these are illusory. A man does not have mastery even
over what he has in hand; if God withholds his capacity to
"enjoy" it, he might as well not own the wealth; never a basis for
the meaning of life, it is "vanity."

The miserable state of one from whom God withholds the
gift of enjoying one's property is pictured by means of an ex-
treme and fantastic example. Koheleth uses the familiar case-
law style: "If" (vs. 3; see Exod. 21:3-14). Children and great
age are the epitome of life in the Old Testament (Gen. 25:8;
35:29; Job 42:16-17). But even a hundred children and "a
thousand years twice told"—the latter beyond the realm of man's
possibility twice over (see Ps. 90:4; Gen. 5:25-27)—could not
give a man "rest" if he could not enjoy them. The lot of such a
man is less attractive than that of an abortion that never saw
the light of day (vss. 3c-5; see 4:2-3). Included in the "enjoyment" of his wealth of children and years would be a man's
burial (vs. 3). In Israel, burial was synonymous with the perpetuation of one's name or memory: a man who was "gathered
to his fathers" enjoyed his "wealth" in this and found "rest." But,
says Koheleth, only God can make this happen, not one's wealth.
Therefore wealth is vanity. And because man can never know
whether God will let it happen for him, man never has "rest";
he is never satisfied. In the Epistle to the Hebrews the faithfulness
of God as such, affirmed in faith, is the source of man's "rest"
(Heb. 4:3). While Koheleth shares the God-centeredness of the
New Testament, he does not share the eschatological viewpoint
of the New Testament which no longer makes faith dependent
upon any specific result outside of God himself.

In 6:7-9 the nature of property is dealt with in three brief
sayings. Modern social psychologists who feature the instinct of
self-preservation, as expressed in the need for food, are fore-

shadowed in verse 7: a man works so that he can eat. Proverbs 16:26 cites the same fact, but as a word of encouragement to the worker. Koheleth cites it to make his oft-repeated point that man can never reach a final goal, whether by work or otherwise. Verse 8 is a question which clearly intends to qualify the distinction between the wise and the foolish and to puncture the pretensions of the former. But the meaning of the second half of the verse is obscure. It seems best to think of "the poor man" as synonymous with the wise; that is, one who may be poor in goods but is not a fool—the "poor in spirit" of the New Testament. The question is not answered because it sums up the whole problem Koheleth has raised. The comparison in verse 9 makes the point that it is better to enjoy the gifts and goods of life one has ("sight of the eyes") than to toil on to increase them ("wandering of desire"), thus summing up the way of life Koheleth repeatedly prescribes as proper, given the fact of the vanity of life (2:24-25; 3:12-13, 22; 5:18-20).

In verses 10-12, concluding the long series of observations on "riches," Koheleth sums up the whole human situation: man is not able to "dispute" with God because God is so infinitely "stronger than he." We may imagine him as reading or hearing Job's long debate with God, or Jeremiah's presentation of his "case" (Jer. 12:1-4), and smiling indulgently as he thinks, "They are asking for the impossible." Indeed, Job (Job 42:1-6) and Jeremiah (Jer. 20:7-9) discovered this for themselves. But neither reacted in the mood of resignation that Koheleth displays when he contemplates the divine sovereignty, which he seems to think of as a series of eternal and static decrees, both unchangeable and unknowable, rather than as a dynamic and creative reality.

What Gives Security? (7:1-14)

In contrast to Proverbs, Koheleth finds it impossible to say who or what is good in an absolute sense. All things are relative, and it is only possible to speak of better and worse. So, in his book, he developed what may be called the "better" saying, in which the quality or value of an action or state is expressed comparatively. Examples of this occur in 2:24; 3:12, 22; 4:6, 9, 13 and 5:5. In this section there are half a dozen examples of this comparative form. They serve well to illustrate a fundamental relation between the literary style and the outlook on life of the author.

The series is evoked by 6:12, "For who knows what is good for man . . . ?" No one knows in any final sense; that, for Koheleth, is central to his experience of the futility of life. However, he is prepared to offer some examples of what is better and so to indicate the direction of his outlook on life. He does so by expanding and editing a series of extant proverbs.

Verse 1a is a saying in the spirit of Proverbs (compare 22:1). A "good name," of course, is something that survives one's death, enhancing one's life. This aspect of it seems to catch Koheleth's fancy, for the meaning he assigns to the fact of death guides his criticism of the sages. It is the fact, above all others, that makes all values relative. Hence, he adds his comment in verse 1b and then in verse 2 creates a second "better" saying, synonymous with the first, to emphasize his point. In verses 3-4 a third saying is offered which in the interpretation provided makes the same point. Proverbs 14:13 states that joy can end in grief; Koheleth says that a somber, realistic appraisal of the facts of life is the basis upon which man must rest whatever joy there is. The goodness of life, such as it is, must be defined in relation to the inescapable fact of death. Hence, "the heart of the wise is in the house of mourning."

The fourth comparison (vss. 5-7) says that it is "better" to hear "the rebuke of the wise" than "the song of fools." Why? For the sages the answer was clear and absolute: because the one led to life and the other to death (see the comment on Prov. 4:10-19). But Koheleth denies that man can find life; learning and wisdom are not an absolute good, only "better." When the writers of Proverbs heard the "song of fools" they lamented the fact that men would forfeit great opportunities; for Koheleth the revelry of the fools is macabre, like a death dance. He is already oppressed to the point of hopelessness by the narrowness of the human situation. The brittle laughter of the fools confirms his gloom. It has for him the crackling sound of the burning thornbush: man is consumed and his life is vanity (vs. 6). The rebuke of the wise can at least make us aware of the real situation we are in, though it cannot change it; it is only "better." Besides, he adds in verse 7, the wise have feet of clay: in moments of persecution they often lack the courage to stand up and be counted (see Prov. 24:10-12), and in temptation they often prove corruptible and accept a bribe. The difference between sage and fool is, after all, quite relative. Koheleth has much in common with our contemporary existentialist writers of the literature of despair, and, like them, he clears the ground for a much deeper grasp of man's sinfulness and helplessness.

The fifth saying (vss. 8-10) in this series in response to the question "What is good?" contains a double comparative (vs. 8). Both the popular wisdom of Israel (I Kings 20:11) and the professional sages agree that "the end" is the thing that matters. The "end" is a goal and is usually thought of as a good thing— a harvest after planting, wisdom after schooling; in such areas the difference between "beginning" and "end" is absolute. But in Koheleth it is only relative ("better"), for *the* end is death; a harvest (or wisdom) is only penultimate. Verse 8 must be read in the light of verse 1. The parallel comparison about the patient and the haughty is closely synonymous: there is no place for officiousness, for man does not determine the end. The sages rejected anger for practical reasons, considering it a fool's desire. Koheleth agrees that anger is foolish (vs. 9) but, as the connection with verse 8 indicates, provides a more profound reason for his judgment. In verse 10 he refutes those who, like romantics in every age, insist that life was better in earlier times. Wisdom teaches us that this is not so, he says. What he means, considering the context, is that people died then also.

In the English text the sixth and last saying (7:11-12) does not give evidence of a comparison. As it stands, verse 11a might give the impression that Koheleth taught that wisdom *without* wealth was not "good," which surely is not the case. The Hebrew for 11a is better translated, "Wisdom is as good as an inheritance." The sages generally said wisdom was better than wealth (Prov. 16:16). This author calls them equal, thus relativizing wisdom; and for good measure he emphasizes that only for "those who see the sun"—that is, for the living—is either of any use. The Hebrew word for "protection" (vs. 12) is literally "shadow," which is used in 6:12 and 8:13 of the transitoriness of man's life. Koheleth seems to have chosen his word with double sense: wisdom and wealth offer protection, but not against death. Both are relative goals.

The conclusion (7:13-14) of this closely reasoned and artfully constructed section consists of two things: (a) an admonition to remember that God is God and that man cannot change his ways or decrees (see 1:15) and (b) a reminder that God ordains both man's prosperity and his adversity. As is frequently the case at the conclusion of a section in his dissertation on the vanity of life, Koheleth here calls men to be "joyful," to enjoy the relative values of life as gifts of God. But in stressing that "the day of adversity" is also "made" by God, including the day of death, he has emphasized the extent to which man must live by faith. God is the only possible object of man's faith.

The Relativity of Righteousness (7:15-22)

This section continues to tussle with the question raised in 6:12. As it is impossible to say how man can make his life secure in an absolute sense (7:1-14), so it is also impossible to say what is righteousness in an absolute sense.

Koheleth cites another example (compare 3:11; 4:1) of the superficiality of the popular piety of the sages: it is not true that the wicked die young or that the righteous always prosper (but see 8:12). Sometimes the reverse is true, though this does not mean that man should reverse his moral understanding. All human valuations of an ethical sort are relative. It is possible to be "righteous overmuch" and to be "wicked overmuch" in the sense that we absolutize and/or oversimplify our definitions of moral good and wickedness. Koheleth has learned that all motives are mixed; also, he senses that the embodiment or result of every deed of man contains possibilities for both good and evil. Nothing is wholly pure, or wholly impure. Koheleth had noticed that sometimes men were destroyed in the name of the good and the true (4:1-3). Here he cautions his readers against becoming crusaders and reformers in the name of some human definition. He has discovered that moralism absolutized can be inimical to the fear of God (vs. 18), for fear of God includes the awareness that he alone can distinguish between right and wrong. This author is an enemy of legalism. Man is saved, if he is saved at all, by the fear of God, not by what he can manage for himself.

In the following verses (19-22) Koheleth applies his view. Having cited a well-known proverb in verse 19, he continues the thought of verse 18 in verse 20: no man is completely righteous. This was generally admitted (I Kings 8:46; Job 15:14-16; Prov. 20:9). But in verses 21-22 Koheleth makes it serve as the basis for mercy and forgiveness toward his fellow man: when a man or slave curses him he does not invoke the punishment of the law in retaliation but remembers how often he has himself

"cursed others." However implicitly, this anticipates the petition
about debts and debtors in the Lord's Prayer (Matt. 6:12; compare Eph. 4:32).

Female Deviousness (7:23-29)

The first two verses of this section, reminiscent of 1:12—2:26
in the role assigned to wisdom, stand as a transition between the
preceding subject and the one that follows.

The wisdom literature of Egypt and the Book of Proverbs
contain both very high and very negative estimates of women
(see Prov. 18:22; 27:15-16; 31:10-31). This is also true of
Koheleth (see 9:9). In 7:23-29 the Preacher's description of a
woman as "snares and nets" is reminiscent of the sections on
the "strange woman" in Proverbs 1-9.

Proverbs 20:6 inquires whether it is possible to find a faithful
man. Koheleth has the same question about women, though pro-
fessing to have found "one man among a thousand" (vs. 28).
Since in verse 29 the author seems to be again preoccupied with
Genesis 1-3, one may ask whether his view of woman is here
influenced by the story of the Fall (see I Tim. 2:14).

In the conclusion of verse 29, with its "they," man and
woman are again treated as equal; both have "sought out many
devices." What Koheleth seems to say is that the sage's attempt
to describe the real meaning of the human situation is always
bound to fail, thanks in part to the inscrutability of man himself.
From 3:16 on, Koheleth has provided illustrations to show that
the human scene is much more complex and ambiguous than
would appear, and not nearly as easy to describe truly as the
popular piety nurtured by the sages assumes. This is one more
in that long series.

The Ruler (8:1-8)

Both in ancient Egypt and in Israel the sages inculcated a
degree of respect and reverence for the king which seems ob-
sequious and servile to us. In Egyptian wisdom especially there
is an abjectness which would make it unlikely that a spirit of
revolution would develop. The attitude in Israel is somewhat
more moderate, but the ethos is similar (see Prov. 20).

In chapter 1, verses 1 and 12, Koheleth impersonates Solomon, but there is no trace of that here. He seems simply to reiterate the view of earlier sages. Verse 4 is a proverb about the absolute finality of the king's word; no one may challenge him. This proverb, with its rhetorical question, stressing the radical separation of ruler and ruled (compare Isa. 45:9-10), seems to be quoted by Koheleth to support the counsel in verses 2-3. The proverb in verse 1, exalting the sage, was probably also an extant saying used by our author. Its relevance becomes apparent when we recall that the king was considered the wise man par excellence, inasmuch as his office and state gave him access to the secrets of God.

The meaning of verse 3 seems clear: one carries out the king's command, however unpleasant; it is dangerous to do or even contemplate otherwise. The precise meaning of verse 2 is very obscure. Partly in the light of verse 3 one is led to the conclusion that what is meant is that one should simply obey and not too quickly complicate one's situation by taking an oath.

While Koheleth endorses the deep reverence for the king taught by the sages, he does so for his own very different reasons. This becomes clear in the last half of the saying, from verse 5 on.

The first half of verse 5 is virtually a quotation of Proverbs 19:16; but the last half is the Preacher's own. What it says is that a wise man is one who knows "of a time and a judgment" (instead of "the time and way"). That is, he knows that God keeps his own counsels (3:1-12) and that he does not share the knowledge of his purposes with mortals. For the sages the power and the wisdom of the king stand as a challenge to moral obedience; for Koheleth it becomes the symbol of God in his mysteriousness.

Having reinterpreted the function of the absolute monarch for his own understanding of the relation between God and man, Koheleth proceeds in the next three verses to reiterate some of its main features: all things have their time, though God alone disposes of this; therefore, man "does not know what is to be," not even the sage. The crowning proof of this incapacity of man is the fact that he has no "authority over the day of death" (vs. 8).

Man's Inhumanity to Man (8:9-15)

This is another little essay in the first person singular, a favorite form for Koheleth, in which he reports on his observations in the empirical world of men and affairs to illustrate his convictions and themes. It is therefore basically separate from the saying that comes just before it and which does not have this feature. However, verse 9 does provide an external tie between the two. The point had just been made that a man does not have "authority" over the day of his death (vs. 8). Yet man "lords it over man" (vs. 9, the same root in Hebrew). Thus the transition is made from the theme of human impotence to that of human injustice. The latter appears ironical in the light of the former.

In his first example Koheleth relates how he witnessed the honorable burial of wicked men and heard them praised in the very city where they had done their evil deeds. The vivid and familiar scene evokes the comment, "This also is vanity." That is, Koheleth sees in this example of obvious moral incongruity another illustration of the inscrutability of the way of God with respect to the human situation. For all man can discover and know, his world is a jungle that offends both his intelligence and his conscience.

In the next three verses (11-13) Koheleth explicitly rejects the logical conclusion that might be drawn from his observation. The world may appear to be a moral jungle, and man cannot prove it is otherwise. The "heart of the sons of men is fully set to do evil" because of this. Yet for Koheleth this conclusion is both cynical and superficial. However long delayed, and whatever the appearances, "it will be well with those who fear God," he insists. In God's time and in his way the moral orderliness of life will be vindicated. Koheleth's confidence in an ultimate vindication of moral responsibility perhaps only seems to stand out more clearly here than elsewhere, because in his characteristically "yes—but" style he here distinguishes himself from those who have abandoned all hope in a moral order of things rather than, as is more commonly the case, from those who are overly confident about being able to demonstrate it as a fact.

The second example (vs. 14) is really an amplification of the first. A general principle is emerging: the wicked prosper and the good suffer. Increasingly, from the time of Ecclesiastes on, poverty, suffering, and weakness came to be seen as marks of the good rather than of the evil (see, for example, Luke 6:20), and this in turn implied a revolutionary development in the Bible's definition of the nature of man's destiny as an eschato-

logical rather than a historical hope. Koheleth announces none
of this, though he unwittingly prepares the way for it. He can
only counsel men again to accept the day with its daily budget
of work, pleasure, and food as the gift of God (vs. 15).

God's Work and Man's Quest (8:16—9:12)

Koheleth returns to a familiar theme in phrases reminiscent
of his treatment of it in 1:12—2:26. In 8:16-17 he states the
whole matter in what amounts to a propositional statement: no
matter how he toils and drives himself, and despite his wisdom,
man cannot discover the ways of God.

Like the sages who wrote Proverbs, Koheleth thought of
all man's life and its activity as a quest. The object of this quest
was to find out the character and implications of "the work of
God"; that is, to learn to know God by studying natural and
historical processes, on the assumption that he is active in these
and is disclosed through them. Proverbs shows that its authors
were convinced that it was possible to discover God in this manner, especially that man could define the meaning and goal of
his own life as a result of this. They held that God revealed
himself in the order of creation and that a disciplined man of
intelligence could apprehend him. A "wise man" was one who
had discovered God in this way. But Koheleth is not certain that
this quest can ever succeed. This he asserts flatly here: even
"the wise man [who] claims to know" does not know and cannot
know; he deludes himself. Koheleth sets himself over against the
authors of Proverbs much as a modern existentialist attacks an
ethical idealist.

Having stated his view that God remains far from man and
does not grant him an insight into his purpose, the Preacher
meditates upon its implications. In 9:1-10 he begins with a
first-person account of the course of his thought. Man "cannot
find out" (8:17); therefore "the righteous and the wise and
their deeds are in the hand of God" (9:1). To be in the hand of
God is here synonymous with not being able to do anything of
one's self. Today when one says, "How are you?" to a Muslim
Arab who is in an extremely bad way economically or physically,
he will reply, "I am on Allah." This may or may not mean that he
puts his trust in God. But what it means first and foremost is
that as far as he himself is concerned he is helpless; there is

nothing he can do. This is Koheleth's point precisely; even "the righteous and the wise," who presume to be able to plan their final goal because they think they have knowledge of God's ways, are helpless. The meaning of their "deeds" is also "in the hand of God." Thus Koheleth reiterates what he said in 8:17b: man cannot "find out" God (see Job 11:7). In our day Christian theologians differ about the extent to which, by science and philosophy, they can achieve an understanding of God that is correlative with the knowledge of him confessed by faith. Koheleth depreciates every possibility of this. The meaning of man's deeds is not at man's disposal, his "deeds are in the hand of God." Man cannot anticipate the "love or hate" that will come from them, or apart from them, from the mysterious action of God. Koheleth's use of such unpredictable phenomena as love and hate (compare II Sam. 13:1-2, 15) serves him well in making his point that for man all of life is unpredictable; it comes from the hand of the unknown God whom man can never know. Hence, everything is "vanity."

Characteristically, at verse 2 the personal statement makes way for a general declaration (vss. 2-6). All men die; "one fate comes to all" (see 2:14; 3:16-21). All distinctions between better and worse and the more or less true as men make these are of relative significance for man's life, for his death wipes them all out. Koheleth utters a revolutionary doctrine that must have shocked many of his fellow Jews, however sophisticated they may have been. For what he says, in effect, is that it makes no difference whether a man is a Jew or a Gentile (compare Rom. 10:12; Gal. 3:28), whether he observes the dietary laws or not, and whether he offers the prescribed sacrifices or not. For Koheleth, as for the New Testament, all human forms and practices are relativized by the fact that God is all, though Koheleth could not add, as does the latter, "and in all."

Death is the great leveler; it mocks all man's pretensions to meaning and dignity. The "one fate" of death touches all he does, so that, despite himself, man's life is always "evil" (that is, "bad," "rough"), and he is foolish even when he seeks wisdom (vs. 3). After meaningless life comes death. Sometimes Koheleth says death is preferable to life (4:1-3), for the dead need no longer witness the inequity and meaninglessness of life. But here he is impressed by what that release implies, the total extinction of consciousness: "the dead know nothing" (vs. 5). A man's life is indeed like that of a dog, the most despised animal in the

Near East; but a living man never ceases to live for tomorrow. He has "hope," even though it is unrealizable. The dead are simply wiped out, the memory of name and monument notwithstanding.

The author concludes his discourse with four admonitions in the imperative (9:7-10). Inasmuch as man's works are in the hand of God and inasmuch as the same fate awaits all men, what must one do? He must become what today's existentialists call the man involved (*l'homme engagé*), the man who throws himself into life without reserve. Koheleth frequently expresses the view that the best thing for man to do is to find satisfaction in work, food, and human companionship (2:24-26; 3:12-13, 22; 5:18-20). Here for the first time he formulates this view in commandments. There is also a new reason to justify the view, because death (Sheol) spells the end of everything. Man must keep busy not just to keep his mind off the evils of this life but because life, such as it is, is so brief.

In verse 7 the author tells his readers that God has already "approved" their work. This must probably be understood in a deterministic sense. Man cannot know the meaning of what he does, good or evil; but God uses it in his own way and for his own purpose, whether it impresses man as good or bad.

Once more, to give further documentation to the proposition in 8:16-17, Koheleth refutes the piously held assumptions of the sages (9:11-12). He reverses a little catalog of so-called axiomatic truths that are as dear to the typical modern as they were to the writers of Proverbs: human prowess does not determine human destiny; there is not always bread for the wise or a reputation for the truly gifted. In any case, "Man proposes but God disposes": this is the meaning of "time and chance." From a purely human point of view, life will always be full of surprises. They will be unwelcome because they bear witness to man's helplessness.

Wisdom Slighted (9:13—10:3)

In this section Koheleth continues his criticism of popularly held convictions about the results wisdom can produce. However, in contrast to 8:16—9:12, he does not relate this explicitly to man's ultimate significance and destiny, but only to practical temporal chances and results.

He cites another "example of wisdom" out of his personal experience. What does he mean by saying it "seemed great" to him? As an example of injustice, because the poor man who by his wisdom saved the city was not remembered? Or, as an example of the superiority of wisdom over power, because one man in his wisdom knew how to defeat an entire army? Is he depressed or elated by the story he tells? As usual, a little of both. This is another paragraph in which the persistent "yes—but" mood of Koheleth comes to the surface; in verses 16-18 there are three of the "better" sayings to show it (see 7:1-14). Yes, "wisdom is better than might," but it is not always rewarded. The quiet word of the wise is "better," but the foolish mob often holds men's attention. Wisdom is "better," but one fool ("sinner") can destroy its possibilities.

Usually, after examining a scene or a problem, Koheleth introduces his view about it with the words "I said to myself" (see 1:16; 2:1, 15). Here, with "I say" in verse 16, the "to myself" is lacking, though it may be implied; Koheleth is seldom a proclaimer. But one is reminded of the "I say unto you" of the teachings of Jesus. Here the "I say" is the bridge by which Koheleth moves from the description of a particular example to the enunciation of general statements.

Verses 1-3 of chapter 10 can be read as continuing the series of general conclusions drawn from the "example" described in 9:14-15. The point of 10:1 repeats that of 9:18: one dead fly mixed in the ointment spoils all of it. Wisdom may be "better," but folly often carries the day!

In 10:2-3 Koheleth seems to cease from this running attack on the popular notions about the efficacy and power of wisdom. "Right" and "left" are used as synonyms for light and darkness (compare 2:14) or right and wrong; and the "fool's heart" is set toward the latter. Every sage has said so for years. Yes, adds Koheleth, even when he is on the road he shows to all that he is a fool. Today this would mean that he is a real threat to those who do have a mind, which is the point Koheleth has been making in 9:18 and 10:1 but which may not be intended here.

Assorted Sayings (10:4-20)

In the sayings that follow, Koheleth continues his endorsement (10:2-3) of many of the traditional views of the wisdom movement. He does this by quoting or editing extant materials; by exalting the wise and deprecating the fool; and, especially, by refraining from discussing his own themes about the impossibility of discovering the way of God and about the relativity of all man's knowledge and value. If Koheleth were a contemporary, one might imagine that these are sayings to be used by a speaker at a high school commencement; he aims here to reinforce purpose rather than to create disillusion.

Verse 4 represents the spirit of Proverbs in every respect. Nothing is more dreadful than the displeasure of a ruler (Prov. 19:12; 20:2). But when his anger touches one, the thing to do is to show "deference." To counterattack or to leave is a mistake; one must sit and take it. "Deference" is one English word for the Hebrew term which literally means "healing." Others are "tranquility" (see Prov. 14:30) and "gentleness" (see Prov. 15:4). In all human relationships deference is prized as a virtue that heals the hurt made by an offense.

In verses 5-7 Koheleth reverts to his favorite habit of citing examples from personal experience. It is evil that fools should occupy high positions and "the rich" humble ones. The rich are the wise, for, like Proverbs, the saying assumes that only the wise become rich. For a rich, wise man to be demoted is as evil as it is for princes to walk when slaves ride. This is also the sentiment of the wisdom movement as a whole (Prov. 30:21-22). Nor, despite his use of the first person, does Koheleth proceed to use this observation about a generally recognized "evil" as an excuse to propound his own peculiar philosophy.

In 10:8-9 there are four examples, identical in literary form. There can be no doubt that they all make the same point. What is it? There are several instances of the digging of a "pit" in which the context makes it very clear that the activity is to be thought of in an evil sense, as an effort to trap someone (Pss. 7:15; 9:15; 57:6; Prov. 26:27). The fact that pits were dug to trap lions (for example, Ezek. 19:4, 8) made the metaphor all the more available as an illustration of sinister purpose. But there is nothing in the context here to indicate that Koheleth wants to make the point that an evil person is caught in his own devices. Nor are the other three parallel lines easily associated with this notion. With respect to the fourth, legal provision was made for the danger inherent in log-splitting (Deut. 19:5). It seems probable, therefore, that the one point made by these four lines is, "Accidents will happen." Man is never safe, not even when he is wholly virtuous.

Wisdom is a tremendous asset. That is the point of the saying in 10:10-11. Its "advantage" or "gain" (1:3) is as great as that of a sharpened axe over a dull one or as that of the serpent charmer who arrives in time over the one who comes after the snake has bitten.

In a saying on the fool (10:12-15) the opening verse is a standard proverb in the form of antithetical parallelism so common in Proverbs (see especially chs. 10-15). It seems probable that Koheleth began his little essay with this as his "text." Thus what he tries to concentrate on is the uselessness of the talk of a fool (see Prov. 14:3), which is all the more obnoxious because there is so much of it (Eccles. 5:1-3). Instead of showing great industry and restraint in talk, as a wise man would, labor tires the fool (vs. 15a). In the saying in verse 14 after the expression "a fool multiplies words," we are introduced to the familiar theme of Koheleth about the inscrutability of the ways of God and man's inability to understand his own situation or predict his future. If these words were actually put here by the author, what he seems to have intended was to make the loquacity of the fool seem all the more grotesque in view of the fact that even a wise man cannot say anything final about the meaning of life. These lines, however, do not fit well in the light of the text in verse 12 and in view of the fact that in this section as a whole Koheleth has desisted from his own themes. There is a real possibility that the author did not originally put these lines here, for they seem to change the subject of the saying.

The beatitude, or blessing, is quite common as a form in the wisdom literature (Prov. 3:13; 8:34; Ps. 1:1). The malediction is not so common (see 4:10), but it is used with great frequency by the prophets (for example, Isa. 5:8-23; 10:1). In 10:16-17 Koheleth uses both in a magnificent contrast. "Woe to you, O land . . ." The whole country suffers when its regime is irresponsible, whether because of a king who is still a minor or because of the lack of discipline in those who do have authority. To "feast in the morning" was a sure characteristic of the dissolute (Isa. 5:11, 22). In contrast, "Happy [blessed] are you, O land . . ." The point is that the king is responsible, though for the sages this was associated with belonging to the nobility (Prov. 19:10; 30:22), for they alone received the training the sages provided. The meaning of "free men" must be understood in an aristocratic sense.

The chapter ends with three proverbs (vss. 18-20) wholly in

keeping with the spirit of and corresponding to the subjects treated by Proverbs: laziness as the cause of destitution (see Prov. 24:30-34); food, drink, and money as the answer to life's everyday needs (Prov. 21:17; see comment); and reverence for the king (Prov. 20:2).

Life as Risk and Possibility (11:1-8)

Koheleth is beginning to sum up his views. He has repeatedly said that, in view of the fact that man cannot know the meaning of his life or alter its course, he must simply grasp each day as it comes along and enjoy it to the full (2:24-26; 3:12-13, 22; 5:18-20). One could conclude from this that he was unwilling to commit himself to serious undertakings whose outcome lay beyond the immediate present. Was his ideal of life simply that of a butterfly, summed up in the slogan "Just for today"? He has sometimes been so understood. But this section refutes such views.

There is a great variety here in the way of literary form: admonitions in the imperative (vss. 1, 2, 6), an address in the second person (vs. 5), a so-called "if clause" designating a particular example (vs. 8), and general statements of a propositional sort derivative from the proverb tradition (vss. 3, 4, 7). Finally, there is Koheleth's motto: "All . . . is vanity." This marks a break, the end of the section. The variety of form and the lack of a clearly continuous argument might suggest that the verses stand together by mere chance, as in 10:4-20. However, in this case it seems possible to show that all relates to a single idea the author wanted to convey.

The first two admonitions are usually read as though they were synonyms: be generous when you are able so that in your day of need others will be generous in turn (compare Luke 16:1-9). This may be the meaning of verse 2, though it is probably nearer the truth to interpret it as the equivalent of "Do not put all your eggs in one basket"; that is, diversify, for no one knows where or in what form evil will come. The first admonition (vs. 1) seems to be derived from sea trade. The word for "cast" is literally "send." There were great risks involved, as well as fortunes to be made, in commerce by water. Life is comparable to this sort of risk and possibility. Men must assume the risks of life, says Koheleth, for these are accompanied by great pos-

sibilities. One must make commitments. But, since one cannot
know the outcome of any venture, it is best to provide for any
contingency.

Even the traditional sages acknowledged that the success of a
plan depended upon the blessing of God (Prov. 10:22) and
that man cannot alter God's plan (Prov. 21:30). Koheleth takes
this with full seriousness, however. There is a relentless and
irrevocable logic about God's hidden plan: the writer compares
it to the clouds which when they are "full" simply must drop
their water, or to the tree which lies where it falls, whether to
north or to south (vs. 3). But "nothing ventured, nothing gained":
a man must stop trying to second-guess life. He must act; those
who want certainty will never begin, much less finish, anything
(vs. 4). Man simply cannot have certainty, because all natural
and social processes are "the work of God," which man can
never know, any more than he can trace the path of the wind
(vs. 5, see margin; compare Prov. 30:4) or know how the bones
of the foetus grow in the womb (see Job 10:10-11; Ps. 139:13;
Isa. 44:24). Let us not ask for impossible guarantees, says the
Preacher; "sow your seed" and gather your harvest (vs. 6). If
one hope is left unrealized, another may make up for it. And, who
knows, perhaps "both alike will be good." Like any good Israelite,
Koheleth says that we must grasp life with both hands. The
material world is good; he believes all is the creation of God
(vs. 7; see 3:11). There is a thrill to life and living; and the very
thought of darkness (vs. 8) makes him savor every minute of
life. Life is full of possibilities, but to those unwilling to live with
the fact of risk and uncertainty they are never available.

Youth and Age (11:9—12:7)

The author has come to his concluding essay. He devotes it
to two extremely common themes of the wisdom movement:
youth and age. He deals with each, however, in a manner calculated to reflect his own special views about the human situation, in contrast to those from whom he borrows his themes.

He begins with youth. The sages were the teachers of youth
who, as shown in Proverbs, addressed their pupils by the familiar
phrase "my son." Koheleth is a critic and essayist who cannot
easily adapt to such familiarity; he never uses the phrase (12:12
is an editor's addition). But here, in 11:9, he approximates it
with his "O young man." He plays the role of a wisdom teacher

before his pupil. But the substance of his counsel is radically different from that of those he imitates. The sages of Proverbs always called to duty, obedience, and discipline: "hear . . . instruction" (Prov. 1:8), "do not forget my teaching" (Prov. 3:1), "be attentive to my words" (Prov. 4:20), "treasure up my commandments" (Prov. 7:1), and so on. Here Koheleth's counsel is all summed up in one word, "Rejoice."

The address to youth begins with a series of admonitions in the imperative: "Rejoice"; do what appeals to you ("the ways of your heart," vs. 9); remove irritation from your mind, pain from your body. The last part of verse 9 comes as an intrusion in this series, with respect to literary style as well as thought. It is in all probability a note made by the editor who added 12:13-14 and who felt that the freedom Koheleth offers youth should at least be accompanied by a warning about responsibility.

But why does Koheleth offer youth such startlingly novel counsel? The conviction on which it is founded is put into words in verse 10b: "youth and the dawn of life are vanity." Here his views about the limitations of life and about the impossibility of discovering the ways of God are applied to education and nurture. One must beware of becoming a slave to duty or making an idol of responsibility, for their potential results are only relative. Koheleth anticipates something of Jesus' attitude toward the Law (Mark 2:27-28).

He adds one more admonition, "Remember also your Creator . . ." (12:1). Though, as we have seen (3:11; 7:29), Koheleth was familiar with Genesis 1, he uses the special word for "Creator" only here; more commonly he referred to God as the one who made all things (3:11; 7:13; 11:5). You "remember" your Creator, he says here, when you recognize that the strength and the enthusiastic eagerness of youth are gifts of God, and when you use them to the full because you know they are very transient (see 4:13-16). The whole question of how one should use them, which preoccupied the sages, is not raised.

There is no formal statement of justification for the admonition in 12:1a, comparable to that in 11:10b for those preceding. But the elaborate section on age serves the same purpose: in youth one must "remember" one's Creator because age with its "evil days" which give one no "pleasure" comes so soon. The emphasis upon the imminence of age is made by the thrice-repeated "before" (vss. 1, 2, 6).

Considering the central role he gives to the fact of death in all his thought, it is not surprising that Koheleth should deal more extensively with age than with youth in this essay. The treatment can be divided into three parts:

1. In verse 2 the picture of age is drawn on the analogy of winter weather. In the Holy Land the skies are persistently cloudy only in winter. In other seasons sun and moon shine brightly; even though there may be a brief shower, they return immediately afterward. But in winter "the clouds return" even "after the rain." Old age is the winter of life, says Koheleth.

2. In verses 3-5a age is described by means of what appears to be an elaborate allegory. The human body is compared to an inhabited house which is under a great threat. The "keepers of the house," representing the arms of the body, tremble; its "strong men," probably the legs, are "bent"; the millstones for the grain have ceased to turn, an allegorical reference to the teeth of the body, "few" in old age; and in this threatened house those looking out of its windows, comparable to eyes of the body, are "dimmed." The doors of the house represent an old man's ears; they are "shut." The "sound of the grinding" may be an allegorical reference to the sound of human conversation; the volume of it has diminished. As in the case of an aged person, the slightest sound ("at the voice of a bird") awakens the inhabitants of this imaginary house. The songbirds in it are "brought low"; the voice of the aged has cracked. Like an aged man the inhabitants in the house are afraid of "high" places and think they see "terrors" in every street. Our look at "the house" seems to end in the garden (vs. 5b): the white blossom of the "almond tree" corresponds to the white hair of the aged; and he "drags" himself along (literally, "tries to bear his burden") like a grasshopper who has overeaten! The clause "desire fails" is an interpretation of the Hebrew which actually says, "The caper berry has fruited." The buds of this plant were used as a taste stimulant. What seems to be said here is that these buds have now disappeared, only the ripe berries remain. That is, there is nothing left to stimulate the taste or desire of the aged. The conclusion of the allegorical picture is given in terms of its real point: "Man goes to his eternal home"; that is, to his grave. Age is the harbinger of death.

3. In verses 6-7 the theme of age as the intimation of death is further intensified. The lamp and the well are persistent symbols of life in the Old Testament. The bowl was the receptacle from which the wick drew its oil; the use of the adjective "golden"

suggests its symbolic function here. Without pitcher or wheel, water cannot be drawn. So the lamp of life is put out and the water of life is exhausted. Koheleth here affirms that "the spirit returns to God" (see 3:21).

Conclusion: The Theme (12:8)

Koheleth ends his work by repeating his theme, "all is vanity" (see 1:2). He has detailed to a considerable extent everything that he includes under this "all": wisdom, power, folly, work, social injustice, property, righteousness, youth, and age, to name but a few. All are vain from man's point of view because they do not show him a way in which he can solve the problem of his own situation. Indeed, Koheleth has concluded that, humanly speaking, there is no solution. He does not doubt that God has one; God knows the "time" for everything, also for man. But what this may be, man cannot know.

Two Postscripts (12:9-14)

Two editors have each added a note to endorse the work of Koheleth and simultaneously make it more acceptable to the wisdom movement as a whole. The first emphasizes that "the Preacher" was not only a sage but also a teacher. He not only criticized the work of others but also wrote "proverbs" of his own. With respect to both truth of content and correctness of form Koheleth is reported to have been a perfectionist: "uprightly [in right form] he wrote words of truth." His book would suggest that this creative work was a minor part of his career, though the editor probably features it because of its public appeal. This editor closes by paying a tribute of his own to the words of "the wise." Probably recalling some of the sharp things Koheleth has said, he compares them to goads; and, he adds, they are all "given by one Shepherd"; that is, they all come from God. Koheleth, of course, had never made this claim for his work, and to do so qualifies his basic thesis that the truth about life, as God sees it, is not divulged to man. But, like any relativist, Koheleth would have insisted, we may suppose, that his discovery that all things are relative is an absolute truth that stands as an exception to the rule that all things are relative.

The second note no longer talks about Koheleth but warns

against certain developments he may have set in motion. It cautions against going "beyond" the collected sayings of the wise, which the first editor cited, to an endless inquiry into such endless riddles as Koheleth points to. It can only weary one and leads to a loss of the simplicity of things more evident in Proverbs. He summarizes the meaning of Koheleth's thought in his own way: "Fear God, and keep his commandments," thus reconciling it with his own point of view, which seems to be substantially the same as that of Proverbs.

THE SONG OF SOLOMON

INTRODUCTION

Character, Literary Form, and Setting

This book is called "The Song of Solomon" or "The Song of Songs," after its opening verse. To designate it as "Solomon's" can mean in Hebrew either that he is its author or that he is the "patron" to whom it is dedicated. The former does not seem likely. It contains the Persian loan word for "paradise" (4:13, "orchard"), which points to a much later era than the time of Solomon. It cites Tirzah (6:4), the first capital of the Northern Kingdom, as the equal of Jerusalem, which would not have been possible in Solomon's time. Even in passages which do reflect the era of Solomon (for example, 3:6-11), and which some would say were composed in his lifetime, the references to Solomon are in the third person, making it difficult to think of him as the author.

To think of Solomon as the patron to whom the book is dedicated is more promising. This serves to bring the book into the circle of the wisdom movement of which Solomon was the founder, the movement which dedicated Proverbs and Ecclesiastes to him. Solomon is credited with having composed over a thousand "songs" (I Kings 4:32), but whether these were of the lyrical sort found in this book we cannot be sure. In both form and spirit this Song of Solomon differs from the didactic emphasis of Proverbs and the analytical reflectiveness of Ecclesiastes. It is lyrical and joyous. It is an emotional outpouring that sings the sensate enjoyment of life for its own sake. History, purpose, duty, and hope are all forgotten; the poet revels in today and in the beauty of the created world for what it is. Ecclesiastes recommended this sort of relishing of life (for example, Eccles. 5:18-19; 9:9-10); here we have an unrehearsed and spontaneous example of it.

There is a third way of understanding the mention of "Solomon" in the title of the book; that is, not as author or patron

but as type or model of the bridegroom, however this bridegroom
is to be conceived. This does not exclude the possibility that the
Song has affinities with the wisdom movement, specifically in
its preoccupation with the order of creation for its own sake; but
it draws attention to the fact that the Song is not focused on
wisdom but on love. It is "Solomon's" Song; that is, the song of
the bridegroom.

Although the book is called a Song, it is better to think of it
as a whole series of songs. Attempts to treat it as a dramatic
poem, which is given unity and progression by a plot, have not
succeeded. What we have is a collection of lyrical songs; some
by the lover, others, somewhat more in number, by his beloved.
Usually each addresses the other, although there are occasional
recitals or soliloquies in which the partner is spoken of in the
third person (for example, 3:1-5). The "daughters of Jerusalem,"
who may be thought of as the attendants of the "bride" or beloved, seem occasionally to serve as a chorus to introduce songs
by means of a question (for example, 5:9; 6:1). The adjuration
that love be given its innings is addressed to them by the bride
(2:7; 3:5; 8:4). The repetition of this adjuration and of other
phrases—such as the title for the beloved, "fairest among women"
(1:8; 5:9; 6:1)—reinforces the unity of the subject matter of
the lyrics by pointing to the utilization of a common stock of
metaphors and themes. Others include: the vineyard (1:6; 2:15;
8:12), the mother's house (3:4; 8:2), the garden (4:12, 15, 16;
5:1; 6:2), and the pasturing of the flock (2:16; 6:3; compare
1:7; 6:2).

The lyrics of this Song, however we define their original
meaning and function, are to a surprising extent reflected in the
Arabic folk songs current in the Near East today, especially in
rural regions. In particular, the contemporary lyrics also perpetuate the descriptions of the lover and the beloved which
strike the westerner as strange (see 1:9-11; 4:1-7; 5:11-16; 6:4-
10; 7:1-9). And it may be added that this sort of description is
demonstrably much older than the Song; examples of it are
found in the love poetry of both Babylonia and Egypt. Considering the persistence of this literary genre, the recognition that in
the Song it utilizes an extant stock of metaphors, and in view of
the fact that the book is not a dramatic entity but a collection
of lyrics that can be extended indefinitely, it becomes impossible
to confine it to a definite period or assign a single author to it.

Purpose

To ask about the purpose of this book is to raise the whole question of the history of its interpretation. We shall look at three ways in which an approach is made to an understanding of the meaning and purpose of the Song of Songs.

The first of these approaches is commonly called the allegorical one. What it assumes is that the apparent meaning and purpose of this book, the celebration of nature and specifically of human love, is not really its meaning or purpose in fact. It assumes that these lyrical songs of love are intended as an allegory, to celebrate the covenanted relationship between God and man. This allegorical interpretation has had a long, continuous, and impressive history. It has been used by Christians as well as Jews and by both Catholics and Protestants.

Rabbi Akiba, who flourished at the end of the first Christian century, described the Song of Solomon as "The Holy of Holies" of the entire Jewish Bible, for it dealt with the mystery of the relationship between God and his chosen people, Israel, not simply with the deeds of God as universal Creator. It should, however, be pointed out that Rabbi Akiba exalted the book to help fix its place in the canon, which was disputed by those who thought it was simply a book about man.

Israel's allegorical interpretation of the Song was a very natural thing, because prophets such as Hosea, Jeremiah, and Ezekiel especially had used the metaphor of God as the husband and Israel as the bride to describe the Covenant. While they usually spoke of a brokenness in the relationship because of the faithlessness of Israel, the bride, there is in Jeremiah 2:2 a touch of the lyrical spirit which pervades the Song of Solomon. There is, moreover, evidence that the tendency to portray sacred objects and relationships in the metaphors of marriage was common in Israel. Thus, beginning with Proverbs, Wisdom is the "bride" men are urged to choose because of her faithfulness; and later both Law and Sabbath are "brides" for the faithful Jew. To read the songs of this book allegorically was, therefore, quite natural; and the fact that in the days of the New Testament this practice was standard procedure shows that it began very early. What *cannot be shown*, however, is that the Song of Solomon was composed to be read in this way.

In Christianity the variety of the allegory increases. Sometimes the lover and his beloved are Christ and the Church. At other times Mary the mother, as the divine Wisdom, is the "bride" of the believer, and the Christ is the "lover" of his soul. A remarkable number of Christian hymns, both ancient and modern, can be shown to have drawn on the allegorical reading of this book for their metaphors. Expository preaching which treated the Song of Songs allegorically was standard in Protestant practice until the end of the nineteenth century, and has not entirely disappeared. The allegorical use of the Song in Catholic piety, immensely enriched by great mystics, continues unabated and with multiple variations in meaning.

Although it cannot be shown that the Song was intended as an allegory by its composers, it is also impossible to point to a time, at its very beginning, when it was understood simply as a poem of human love. The first intimations of this known to us occur as a minority voice in the day of Rabbi Akiba; and they do not persist. Not until modern times, with the rise of systematic literary and historical analysis, did the natural, human interpretation of the Song gain the ascendancy.

According to this second approach the purpose of the book is to celebrate human love. This view sees the book as a collection of wedding songs, composed for and used at the lengthy wedding festivities which played a large role in the folk culture of ancient Israel, as among the Arab peasantry today. The wedding songs current among these people, as already noted, show remarkable similarity in spirit, style, and vocabulary to the Song of Solomon.

The last two hundred years of study have made quite clear that the Song is certainly not exclusively preoccupied with the relation between God and man, as the allegorical approach assumed. It is concerned about human relations, especially about the relation between man and woman. But we may not conclude therefrom that it is not concerned about the relation between God and man. The people who wrote the Bible had no equivalent for our notion of the "secular"; they did not separate the natural from the sacred as we often do, for they took very seriously their confession of God as Creator of all.

The third approach to understanding the purpose and meaning of the Song is the most recent of all. This approach assumes that the roots of the Song are fixed in the cult liturgies of ancient, pre-Israelite Canaan and that the songs are adaptations from the rites built upon the ancient myths of this religion. This approach helps us to get at some of the truth about the Song. It has shown that there are echoes of the fertility religion of Canaan in these songs, echoes that are expressed in motifs, vocabulary, and titles. It is safer to speak about echoes of a myth and its cultic poems than to speak of the Song as an adaptation of a specific cultic liturgy. That is, the composers of the songs were shaped by a milieu and drew their language from a cultural setting in which the cultural and religious legacy of ancient Canaan was in solution. They were not trying to preserve, rescue, or adapt ancient liturgies; they were not even conscious of those liturgies as such, for they had been dissolved and assimilated. This legacy of Canaan had become a part of Israel's own culture, much as the Greek legacy has entered into ours.

Inasmuch as the Song utilizes materials that were once put to a religious use, honoring a human "bride" with exalted language first phrased to honor "the queen of heaven," its availability for allegorical and mystical purposes is enhanced. The study of the history of religions has made it very clear that, phenomenologically speaking, both Jewish and Christian piety owe a great deal to the Canaanite legacy. In part this is mediated and made available through the Song of Solomon, a song about human love and the beauty of creation which simultaneously and, we believe, providentially served as the solvent for the assimilation of a great cultural legacy. Thus it must be said that we cannot single out any one of these three approaches to the Song as the clue to our understanding of its meaning; they all contribute to it.

Message

This book does not talk about God or about his deeds. It never mentions God. It does not talk about "the human situation" as a problem—about sin, duty, weakness, death, or salvation. It does not even discuss creation. It simply assumes it and sings about it. Its stance is lyrical. Its expressions are entirely spontaneous. It responds to all the stimuli of nature and, in particular, it puts into words the reactions produced by the aroused impulses of desire. It is a sensate and sensuous book in every respect. In this it does not differ basically from the Old Testament—or from the Bible— as a whole. It is distinctive only in the mode in which it expresses this wholehearted involvement in nature and matter; that is, in man's enjoyment of it. The "message" of this book relates to the meaning of creation: it is to be enjoyed.

What impresses the thoughtful reader of the Song of Solomon is that its composers respected nature, notably as expressed in human beings, and knew how to savor it. Indeed, it is this savoring of natural life—rather than the possession and use of it, much less the misuse or abuse of it—around which the Song revolves. Its respect for life is expressed in the savoring of it; and it is this that makes it a very important commentary on the meaning of the confession that God is the Creator of all things. The presence of the Song in Scripture is a most forceful reminder that to confess God as Creator of all things visible and invisible is to deny that anything is "common" (see Acts 10:9-16) or, to use the cliché of today, "secular." This book teaches that all life is holy, not because we, as Christians, make it so, but because it is made and used by the living God.

OUTLINE

COMMENTARY

The Superscription (1:1)

The title treats the book as a single song, although it is better thought of as a whole series of songs with a single theme. It is a "Song of Songs"; that is, the most beautiful of songs, or songs on the most beautiful of themes (compare "King of kings"). The relative pronoun "which" has a form different in Hebrew from the one used consistently elsewhere in this book, which supports the view that this title sentence is provided by an editor. The possessive "Solomon's" could mean that the editor considered Solomon the author; but it can also mean that he dedicated the poem to Solomon. The case is the same as that of the frequent superscription "a Psalm of David" in the Psalter. This dedication has the effect of relating the book to the wisdom movement. Solomon was credited with having produced songs as well as proverbs (I Kings 4:32).

An Invitation to Love (1:2-4)

In this song, as very often in the book, the woman, or "bride," plays the leading role. She is the speaker in verses 2-4a. With ardent desire she addresses "the king," praising his "name" (that is, his character), yearning for his embrace, and literally commanding him to take her with him ("draw" in verse 4 can also mean "drag" or "pull"). Finally her goal is reached, she announces that they are in the king's chambers. Then (vs. 4b), using the plural number associated with majesty, the king addresses the woman, declaring that the eagerness is mutual; he will extol her love "more than wine" (compare vs. 2b). The closing line is again spoken by the bride and echoes the close of verse 3; it may be an addition.

Who is this "king"? Is this God, whose bride is Israel? (Jer. 2:2). Is this Christ, whose bride is the "new Jerusalem," the Church (Rev. 21:2, 9), or the soul of the believer? That is the traditional allegorical or mystical view.

Or is this "king" simply a title of honor for a young husband during his festal marriage week? And is this song a song of human love recited at such festivities? That is the view of those who treat this book as a collection of folk songs dealing with love and marriage.

Again we may ask: Is this "king," at least originally, an earthly monarch, such as Solomon, who is the "son of God" (see II Sam. 7:14; Ps. 2), his vicegerent on earth? Is the song an echo of a sacred marriage rite in which, playing the role of the deity, the king cohabited with a designated "queen," as a prayer or proclamation that God might fructify the earth and its creatures? That is the view of those who locate the origins of these songs in the cultic practices of the ancient Near East.

There is something to be said for as well as against each of these three interpretations. Though the metaphor of bride and groom as the relationship between Israel and God is very prominent, especially in the prophetic literature, what is lacking in this book, throughout, is any explicit reference to the Deity. Further, while there is ample evidence, in terms of modern as well as ancient parables, to show that these songs were used at wedding celebrations, they nevertheless contain features and emphases—the initiative of the bride, the metaphor of king and court—not easily reconciled with a simple genre of "profane" romantic poetry. Finally, while some of the aspects of vocabulary and metaphor in these songs point to a cultic setting as their locus of origin, it is really not possible to speak of the songs as such as liturgical pieces, whatever echoes of liturgy there may be. History, form, and function of these songs remind us that our distinctions between sacred and secular do not fit the world of experience recorded in Scripture.

Keeper of the Vineyards (1:5-6)

Taken in a purely natural and human way this embodies the Cinderella motif. A charming but sunburned maiden, black as the goats'-hair tents of the nomads, tells the story of how her brothers, in anger, made her keeper of the vineyards. So she could not tend the "vineyard" of her own charm. The motif and the metaphors are common in the love songs of the Holy Land to this day. This is a beautiful bit of romantic poetry. But where do the metaphors come from? And what was the range of their connotations to the earliest readers of this collection? Very early, Israel is described as the "vineyard" of the Lord (Isa. 5:1-7) and he is the "keeper" (Isa. 27:2-3). And in many cases these

metaphors about the relation between God and his people are
drawn from very ancient myths and liturgies indigenous to
Canaan long before Israel arrived on the scene. An ancient
Egyptian writing, for example, speaks of "the maiden" at Jaffa
who guards the vineyards and safeguards her companionship
and charm for her callers.

Where Is the Shepherd? (1:7-8)

In the ancient myth of Ishtar and Tammuz, Ishtar's search
for her brother-husband, dead and lost in the underworld,
is an important feature. The theme of seeking—and of finding—
is also a very prominent one in these songs. Here the maiden
asks where the shepherd she loves pastures his flocks. The
phrase "my soul," used often, is simply a poetic equivalent for
"I." There are many "shepherds," but only one matters to her.
The Lord as the true Shepherd was a favorite religious theme in
Israel (see Ps. 23), and the allegorical possibilities of a verse such
as this must have been evident from the beginning, as in the
case of much folk singing today.

The "answer" is not clear; nor is it clear who gives it. What
it seems to say is that she will find him if she will but perform her
own task, pasture her own flock of little goats, following the
trails of the shepherds camping beside their shelters. But this
may also be the shepherd's way of saying that she is his "pasture" (see 6:2-3). The use of the phrase "fairest among women"
(vs. 8) seems to be a cultic echo that harks back to the golden
Ishtar (see also 5:9; 6:1).

A Dialogue (1:9—2:7)

Here we have a song in antiphonal style in which the lover
and his beloved alternate. He begins (1:9-11) and addresses
her as "my love"; the term literally means "companion," but
its use is limited to this book and it has the same special meaning
in every case (1:15; 2:2, 10, 13; 4:1, 7; 5:2; 6:4). As in the
Arab world today, the horse was prized as a creature of grace,
beauty, and spirit. These are the attributes the lover seeks to
celebrate in his beloved, and she will be honored for these in the
jewels he proposes to give her. The use of what are, to us,
clumsy physical comparisons to point to invisible gifts of char-

acter and personality is a feature of Semitic poetry in general that occurs often in the Song of Solomon.

In her response (1:12-14) the woman again designates her beloved as "the king." The aim of her song is to tell how powerfully and fragrantly attractive she finds him. At a festal meal ("on his couch"), in his near presence, his impact upon her was simply overwhelming. This is really what she means when she says that *her* nard "gave forth its fragrance" or that he was to her "a bag of myrrh" or "a cluster of henna," both highly aromatic substances. As before, physical comparisons serve to get at an invisible dimension in the relationship: his influence upon her is irrepressible, strong, inescapable—and as delightful as perfume. It reminds her of the fragrance of a blooming oasis, such as En-gedi.

The lover responds with only a simple line (vs. 15). He compares her eyes with those of a dove, the intention being to say, no doubt, that she is a lively, sparkling personality and that her eyes show it. It must also be noted that in the ancient Near East the dove was a symbol of the goddess of love, and that in the New Testament it is a symbol of the Holy Spirit (Matt. 3:16).

The beloved responds (1:16), repeating the address "you are beautiful"; and she adds, "lovely," an epithet used in other literature for the gods Ishtar and Adonis. Then she speaks of "our couch" and "our house." The meaning is, "we are well-matched"; "we belong together." But the metaphors also allude to specific marriage customs. Attempts have been made to make the verses refer to a site in the open woods. More probably they refer to a structure especially constructed for the consummation of a marriage, a custom of which fragmentary parts survive in the Near East even today. The need for a special structure was probably rooted in the fact that in ancient cultic practice the "sacred marriage" rite was performed in a special structure. Cedar, which virtually enjoyed a sacred status, was the wood often used for such structures.

The lady ends her song about "our house." There is a break in the dialogue. Then it is she who begins anew with the announcement that she is a "rose of Sharon," and a "lily," which elicits the response from her lover that, among the "maidens," she is like a lily among thorns. Sharon is the seacoast plain of the Holy Land, south of Carmel. Although a profusion of flowers burst out there in the spring, verse 2 makes clear that the point here is the uniqueness of one of these. Indeed, as the allegorists have done when they have applied this metaphor to Israel, Jesus, Mary, or to the Church, it is possible to use the definite article for both the "crocus" (2:1, see margin) and the lily. Both plants are associated with moist places. Reference to the lily occurs frequently in these songs (2:16; 4:5; 6:2, 3; 7:2) and also in Psalm titles (Pss. 45; 69; 80). The lily also figures widely in ancient cultic materials as an erotic symbol, and there it connotes fertility. The varied and wide role that the rose and the lily continue to play in both synagogue and church serves to remind us that the allegorists and mystics perpetuate the metaphors and symbols of ancient cults by re-using them in refined and sublimated fashion. The natural, human connotation given to these metaphors, such as is dominant in the Song of Songs, at least explicitly, is best understood as a stage in this reconception.

In 2:3 the bride tries to match the lover's proclamation of her uniqueness (vs. 2) by asserting that as the fruit-bearing apple tree differs from the trees of the forest, so her lover is distinctive among the "young men." The occurrence of this phrase, as that of the "maidens" in verse 2, may be an example of the cultic legacy in these poems, for the votaries of Tammuz and Ishtar were respectively designated by the technical terms "sons" and "daughters." As in the second song in this dialogue (1:12-14), the bride sets forth the meaning of the relationship with her beloved by means of a physical description that creates an impression: the apple tree gives shade and she likes its fruit. That is, the beloved offers the promise of protection and enjoyment. The security and the sweetness of the relationship for its own sake are celebrated. Though "fruit" often alludes to offspring (for example, Gen. 30:2; Deut. 7:13), it would not be wise, considering the nature of the poetic symbolism, to suppose there is such an intimation here. It may incidentally be noted that the whole matter of procreation and offspring is never touched upon in this book, a fact which distinguishes it from the marriage song proper (see Ps. 45).

What follows (2:4-7) is the account of a love tryst in "the banqueting house," which is, literally, "the house of wine," that is, house of love. Although the poem is a continuation of verse 3, the scene is anticipated by 1:17. The mood is passionate and the imagery highly erotic. Wine and cakes of raisins were used at the orgiastic feasts celebrated in Canaan in honor of the goddess of fertility (Hosea 3:1; see also Jer. 7:18; 44:17-19). In calling for these the bride really calls for the consummation of her union with the lover, not for food; this is implied by the phrase "sick with love" (see 5:8). We should probably read 2:6 as a declaration of this consummation, rather than as the wish for it. This verse recurs in 8:3. Moreover, it corresponds almost literally to a line in the liturgy celebrating the union of the gods Ishtar and Tammuz. That union, celebrated annually, was an aspect of the native mysticism of the Near East, to celebrate and promote fertility and life.

Now the bride makes a solemn appeal to "the daughters of Jerusalem" not to disturb love "until it please." This appeal recurs in 3:5 and 8:4 and is thus also a stock item whose antecedents are probably liturgical. It must be noted that "love" is treated as a quasi-personal reality with a course and end of its own. The sacred marriage represented a most solemn cultic moment, and this appeal may reflect that. The highly cultic and liturgical character of this song in no way denies its role as a song to celebrate an ordinary human union. It is to be noted that in the culture from which such lines were derived every marriage was sacral; that is, it imitated the gods. Israel's monotheism "desacralized" sexual union; it no longer had its prototype in the actions of deity. But it retained its transcendent significance, and so its mystery and awe, because God had created and ordained it (Gen. 1:27-28). In becoming a wholly human thing, as in the Song of Solomon, it did not thereby become profane. That also explains why the Song was so easily utilized by allegorists and mystics.

Herald of Spring (2:8-15)

This song is sung by the bride; but for the most part (vss. 10-14) it is a recitation of the message brought by her lover. He comes as a herald of good news, beautiful "upon the mountains" (compare Isa. 52:7), and he announces that spring has come. He peeks in at the lattice of his beloved's house and tells her the news: sunshine, flowers, the fragrance of orchards in bloom, and the cooing of birds. Nature is alive again. The point of his announcement is made at its beginning and close (vss. 10, 13): "Arise . . . come away." Doves dwelt in the walls of cliffs (Jer.

48:28). The lover wants to see and hear his beloved; he wants her to come to the lattice. He is not comparing her dwelling to a rock but her to a dove. Hence the description of the dove's haunts.

Foxes eat grapes and spoil the vineyards (vs. 15). But it is not clear who is speaking. Is this a continuation of the lover's call, and is he asking his beloved to come and help protect the vineyards, incidentally affording him opportunity to court her? Or are we to think of her as no ordinary maiden but a priestess-guardian of vineyards? (See 1:5-6.) But what if the woman is speaking? How then define vineyards "in blossom"? As the bride's readiness for marital union? And are the foxes those who threaten her integrity? Or, as some interpreters suggest, are they the ravages of time? No really satisfactory interpretation of verse 15 seems to exist.

The Tryst (2:16-17)

This is a very intimate song of an all-night tryst. If we took it as a continuation of the preceding song, as is sometimes done, we could imagine that the bride has admitted her lover to the house for the night. There is a reciprocity about their union comparable to the relation between God and Israel (Lev. 26:12); it is thus not remarkable that verse 16a has been a favorite for Christian mystics. Even more than most, this song combines delicacy with simplicity. Thus the lover's pasturing his flock (see 1:7) is clearly a paraphrase for his enjoyment of his beloved's charms. And, as usual, she takes the initiative, for the imperative "turn" must be read as an invitation to him to indulge his desire for love while the night lasts. Caught by the breaking in of spring, his ardor and eagerness were evident when he came leaping "upon the mountains" (2:8) like a gazelle or a young stag. The song refers to the gazelle and stag once more. What the beloved means is, let this ardor and eagerness have its complete fulfillment.

The Lost Bridegroom (3:1-5)

This song is a beautiful story of alarming loss, dangerous search, and recovery. In the middle of the night the bride discovers that her bridegroom is absent. In terror she gets up to hunt for him in the dark streets of the city. She makes inquiry of the night watchman. Then she finds the one she loves and leads him back to her "mother's house." Reunited with her lover, she closes the song with the refrainlike plea not to disturb "love" (see 2:7; 8:4).

This song has been a great favorite for Christian mystics, such as St. John of the Cross. It serves them as a means of portraying "the dark night of the soul" in which man experiences his alienation from God—the cry of despair from the soul that rises when it learns that the divine fellowship, on which its security rested, no longer exists; and also to portray the soul's search for God, its reconciliation with him, and the union in which it is then bound to him. The pain of alienation and broken fellowship between God and man thus imputed to the poem has its explicit equivalent in Psalm 42.

While the song lends itself in a happy way to this devotional use, it seems probable that initially it alluded to the experience of human lovers. Yet when read as a piece that grows exclusively out of such experience it creates great difficulty for its interpreters. Thus, some treat it as a bad dream of the young bride. But it is not presented as a dream. Moreover, if it were, at what point does the dream recital end, at the beginning or at the close of verse 4? Others, also seeking to account for it as exclusively the experience of human lovers, attempt to treat it in more literal fashion: the bride actually goes out into the dark city to seek the one she loves. This seems even more unlikely; in the Orient, women did not frequent the streets at night and talk to policemen. Besides, why was the bridegroom absent?

The central motif of the song is that of loss, search, and recovery. The whole matter of its interpretation becomes much easier when we read it as an echo of this theme and of the mythological imagery in which it was presented in the cultic legends of the nature mysticism in the ancient Near East. In the Tammuz-Ishtar myth, and in such parallels to it as the Baal-Anath or Osiris-Isis myths, Tammuz, brother-husband of the goddess Ishtar, is annually slain and taken to the underworld. His death and separation from his "bride" cause drought and loss of fertility on earth. But Ishtar goes to the underworld in search of him. As she enters its portals she has an exchange with the "watchmen" who stand on guard there. She finds Tammuz, effects his release, and brings him back to life. With his resurrection and reunion with Ishtar, his bride, fertility and life are restored to the earth; rain falls, plants grow again, and progeny in conceived. The myth, of course, is a reflection of the annual two-season cycle of drought and growth characteristic of that part of the world. Its various aspects were set forth in specific cultic rites in the native religions of the Near East, such as Baalism in Canaan. A Canaanite rite setting forth the search for the lost god-husband is clearly reflected in Hosea 2:7; and the theme of his "return," with the attendant rains, is applied to the Lord of Israel in Hosea 6:3.

This background greatly clarifies our understanding of this song. It is, indeed, a song of human love. By virtue of this it has a lyrical quality which should rule out pedantic attempts to read it as a report of either a specific dream or a search. As a lyric of love and human experience, it utilizes ancient mythological and cultic phrases to carry the impressions it seeks to convey. We must not rule out the possibility that in Israel, as represented by the Song of Songs, this sort of utilization may have involved some assimilation of the Canaanite legacy to Israel's faith and culture, for this book must be viewed as the product of a folk culture. The sacred, the aesthetic, and the human are held together much more closely in the world of the Old Testament than among us.

Solomon's Wedding Day (3:6-11)

This song must be compared with Psalm 45, especially with verses 2-9. It is possible to imagine that it is recited by the beloved about her lover, especially since it is always she who addresses "the daughters of Jerusalem," although here, as a single exception, we also have "daughters of Zion" (vs. 11).

In verse 11 there is an allusion to the crowning of Solomon on his wedding day. This crown or wreath, we learn, was placed upon his head by his mother. The role of the king's mother was extremely important. The story of the succession of Solomon to David's throne (I Kings 1:9-31; 2:13-25) shows this, as does the custom in the Book of Kings of citing the name of the king's mother in the account of his accession. Here the queen mother is given a special role in a royal wedding. It has been suggested that just as in the Near East the king represented the god on earth, so the queen mother represented the goddess; and that the prominence of the queen mother in Israel was related to this custom, even though the God of Israel had no consort.

This song about Solomon's wedding very probably had as its real hero the actual bridegroom at any wedding at which it was sung. It is this song, especially, which is cited by those who see in the Song of Songs a collection of folk songs used by the peasantry to celebrate village weddings. Such festivities last for a week. Banqueting, feats of physical prowess, and recitals are featured, all to honor the couple who are treated as king and queen for the week.

As a song about Solomon's wedding it portrays him as coming "up from the wilderness." There is an honor guard of sixty men and a litter with a richly upholstered palanquin. We are led to believe (vs. 11), it seems, that Solomon came in it, though it would be more in keeping with oriental custom if we thought of this litter as having come to carry the bride from her parental house to that of the groom. It is just possible that the poem intends to portray the arrival of a bride for Solomon. Solomon's harem must have included many daughters of dependent princelings and desert chieftains. The coming of such a festal entourage as is here portrayed must have been a familiar feature of his reign. It does not seem probable that it was a religious processional celebrating the coming of God from Sinai, as has been suggested by some. This is clearly a wedding song that gets its inspiration from the traditions about the splendors of Solomon. And it has a single point: every bridegroom is a Solomon for a week.

The Bride's Beauty (4:1-7)

This description of the bride has parallels in 6:4-10 and 7:1-9, though as a literary category it constitutes a purer example; it is simply a series of similes uninterrupted by other literary forms. Equally pure is the example giving a description of the groom (5:11-16).

As already indicated (see the comment on 1:9-10), these "descriptions" seek to convey an impression about the intangible qualities of the person in question by elaborating the descriptive account of whatever creature or object has been chosen to illustrate it. Modern Arabic love poetry, as well as the love poems of ancient Egypt and Canaan, also utilizes this device.

The lady's eyes sparkle. Her black locks cascade down her shoulders. She shows perfect rows of glistening teeth, chaste scarlet lips, cheeks of russet tan, and she has a royal bearing. The description conveys the impression of a vital, lively, and healthy young woman, an attractive brunette. The lover sums it up in his own way: "there is no flaw in you" (vs. 7).

The important thing to notice is that the poet-lover is seeking to create an impression about his beloved, not to provide a photograph; and he goes about it by describing scenes and objects familiar to his readers. Imagine the reddish-brown of the pomegranate on a person's cheeks. The impression of smooth, clear skin and health is inescapable. Or the armory in "the tower of David," with its austere quiet and great memories; regal bearing and dignity fit such a scene.

The Garden of Love (4:8—5:1)

This section, consisting of antiphonal selections, is marked off by the fact that only here is the beloved addressed as "bride." Coupled with this is the title "sister," which was a characteristic usage in Egypt. The songs sing about the promise of love and its consummation, and for the most part this is presented under the metaphor of a garden. The beauty of the oriental garden, particularly of the Persian garden—and the Persian word "paradise" occurs in verse 13 ("orchard")—is proverbial. Outside there is dry barrenness and burning heat. But the garden is a vine-covered, walled enclosure, irrigated from sparkling fountains, planted with fruit trees, aromatic herbs and shrubs, and flowers arranged in formal design. Here is refreshment, feasting, and the fullness of expansive satisfaction which were later to serve Islamic poets as a model for the fulfillment of heaven. It is a quality of all such poetry, very conspicuous here, that it is highly sensuous without being sensual. The poet knows how to savor life, as well as how to use it; and the former precedes the latter. Though barely alluding to it as such, this book really knows the meaning of the biblical doctrine of creation. It is not an example of grabbing at life, but of a respect for it; such respect is essential for appreciative enjoyment.

The first song (vs. 8) is simply a call. The lover asks his "bride" to leave those mountain ranges to the north which we call the Lebanon and the Anti-Lebanon, and the great peak

Hermon ("Senir"; see Deut. 3:9) at the southern end of the former. Why does this poem feature Hermon? Most probably because according to ancient tradition it was the seat of the goddess of love, Ishtar. Jeremiah calls her the "inhabitant of Lebanon" (Jer. 22:23) and portrays her discomfiture when God comes to judge his people for having forsaken him to follow her. This song stems from a later era when these traditions of the goddess of Lebanon could serve a romantic theme and no longer tempted Israelites to apostasy.

The lover sings again (vss. 9-11). The "bride" has put a spell on him; that is the real meaning of "ravished my heart," which uses a word also used for the cakes baked by Tamar for the inflamed Amnon (II Sam. 13:6). One glance from her makes him helpless. Her love is to him "better . . . than wine" (vs. 10); milk and honey are under her tongue (vs. 11). The meaning is identical despite the contrast in style: she is as good as the best—and better.

Now the lover proceeds to compare his bride to a garden. The metaphor may here have cultic and mythological overtones. The poet has been drawing on the traditions of the goddess of Lebanon, the goddess of love. The seacoast region to the west was the site of the so-called "garden of Adonis," whose annual death was mourned by the women in a special rite that seems to have involved the setting out of "pleasant plants" (Isa. 1:29; 17:10). The great variety of plants our singer ascribes to his "garden" may owe something to such traditions.

Now the bride sings (vs. 16) a delicate little song invoking the winds to carry the fragrance of the garden to her lover so that he may come to it. This is her invitation in response to his in verse 8. She is the pure bride, the virginal "garden locked" (vs. 12), who invites her one and only beloved.

The lover responds (5:1). He is coming to his garden. The thought of the wedding feast prompts the closing lines; all share in the banquet of life set in the garden of love.

The Bridegroom: Three Songs (5:2—6:3)

The three songs in this section (5:2-8, 10-16; 6:2-3) are given continuity by the questions that mark the transitions (5:9; 6:1). That they are actually an organic unity seems rather doubtful. In the first the bridegroom is lost; in the second he is united with his beloved, although there has been no report of his return. Moreover, the second song is a "description" with its own characteristic form (compare 4:1-7).

The first song must be compared with that of the lost bridegroom in 3:1-5. Much of the exposition of that one applies here. Such comparison intimates that perhaps many other songs in this collection, as well as these two, draw on an established stock of motifs and illustrations, varying the use of these to suit individual taste and purpose. The bride's concern for the presence of her lover and her initiative in admitting or seeking him are themes common to both songs, though used differently. The "watchmen" also appear in both, but do not play the same role. Perhaps the clearest illustrations of variations in relation to a common stock is provided by the fact that the oath required of the "daughters of Jerusalem" here takes a different turn (compare 2:7; 3:5; 8:4), in keeping with the fact that the groom is missing. Yet the stock form is clearly in mind and is used to the extent the context permits.

The Christian use of this song to illustrate the call of Christ begins in the New Testament. In Revelation 3:20 we read, "Behold, I stand at the door and knock . . ." This call constitutes the one instance in which the New Testament clearly uses the Song of Songs. It may be noted, incidentally, that the "feast of life" symbolized by the wedding banquet (5:1) is also utilized in Revelation 3:20; it becomes the familiar Messianic feast of Israel's hope. In New Testament times Jewish use of the Song of Songs as a type for the Covenant between God and Israel was, of course, already common. The early Christians adopted this for their own purposes: not God but Christ is the Bridegroom; and the soul of every believer, as well as the Church as a whole, is the bride.

Revelation 3:20 is the one clear example of the New Testament's use of the Song of Songs, but there are other allusions as well. Jesus' saying (Mark 2:19-20) that he, the bridegroom, would be taken away and that then the wedding guests would fast, very probably also has this same song in mind. The story of the five foolish virgins (Matt. 25:1-13), though more doubtful, may also be considered.

That verse 9 was specifically intended to serve as a bridge is indicated by the fact that its second question alludes once more to the oath the bride has exacted from the "daughters of Jerusalem." Moreover, the first question is answered by the description of the second song.

As a literary piece the "description" of the bridegroom corresponds to that of the bride (4:1-7; see comment). As there, the impression created by the objects described gives an intimation of the impact of the lover upon his beloved. For example, the "rounded gold, set with jewels" (vs. 14) must not be read as an attempt to delineate the contour of the bridegroom's "arms" (literally, "hands"). Rather, his hands are said to give the impression created by an artistic piece of gold with jeweled inlay. Did this betoken perfectness of shape, aesthetic sensitivity, or strength? We may not be able to decide in each case, but this should be the approach. To take another example, it would be absurd to point out a *physical* similarity between a man's legs and "alabaster columns set upon bases of gold" (vs. 15a), but as an illustration of the impression of symmetry, harmony, or exquisite proportional relationship the comparison is eminently sensible. The point is driven home by the last half of the same verse. A man could not possibly appear like a mountain range with a cedar forest on it—not physically. But the range of Lebanon, of storied renown in Israel, with its ancient, rare, and fragrant cedars, had created an impression upon this singer that reminded her of her lover. She even gives us a clue: "choice" represents a Hebrew word used constantly of a young man in the prime of his virile strength.

It must be noted that the account of the bridegroom does not consist entirely of a description of other objects for the sake of the impression they convey. In verse 10 the maiden looks directly at her lover: his skin is clear, "radiant" (or "white"; see Lam. 4:7) and "ruddy"; he is a real prince. And in verse 16 she tells us that he is "altogether desirable"; she has found his "kisses" sweet (instead of "speech"; see 2:3 and 7:9). He is a man with a princely face (vs. 10) and noble head (vs. 11), with a quick intelligence (vs. 12); she finds him physically attractive, sensitive (vs. 13), strong (vs. 14), and magnificently proportioned (vs. 15). He is "choice" (vs. 15), "desirable" in every respect (vs. 16). This is her reply to the "daughters of Jerusalem."

In 6:1 we have another transition; the "daughters" ask more questions: Where is he? Can we help you find him? The question assumes that he is still "lost." But the song that follows (6:2-3) bespeaks the union of the lover with his beloved. This is his garden; and to pasture "his flock among the lilies" is a metaphor for their union (compare 2:16-17; also 4:6, 12-15; 5:1). We must therefore conclude either that this little song of intimacy is not the answer to the question asked in 6:1—that is, that its location here is an accident—or that it represents a touch of light-hearted humor. The latter seems possible, considering the imaginative character of lyrical poetry. The maidens ask if they can help their lady find him! What? Find the bridegroom with whom she is united? Of course this assumes that his "return" after 5:2-8 is unrecorded. But considering the nature of this sort of poetry, that is not amazing. These songs are not diaries but episodes to mirror the volatile, intense and vivid, but passing subjective states and impressions of people in love. Logical continuity plays little or no role.

The Bride: Beautiful and Formidable (6:4-10)

This song by the lover opens and closes with the tag that describes his bride as "terrible as an army with banners." He asks her to turn her eyes away from him; they intimidate him. We are led to suppose that she did so, for in verses 5b-7 we find a description of the bride in which the note of alarm is absent. It reiterates part of the description in 4:1-7 (4:1b-2, 3b).

When we read this as a romantic poem it is natural to interpret the formidable aspect of the lady as an index to her feminine purity. She virtually radiates it and confuses all who do not fully appreciate or respect it (see 4:12). However, the metaphors in which this sternness and purity are presented are arresting. They all come together in verse 10: she looks forth (or down) like "the dawn"; she is "fair as the moon" (literally, "the white one") and "bright" (literally, "pure," "clean") as the sun; and she is like an army. Ishtar, the goddess of love, was compared to the pale moon in beauty; but she was likewise a goddess of war, the slayer of men. There can be no doubt that though the song lauds a human bride for her dignity and purity, it does so in phrases and metaphors once used to hymn a goddess of love and war.

This one maiden is incomparable, unique (vss. 8-9). Queens and concubines—an allusion to Solomon's harem—praise her and the maidens call her "happy" or blessed; the word is the one

used for beatitudes (see Prov. 20:7; Eccles. 10:17; Matt. 5:3-11).
In the eyes of her mother, most exacting of all, she is "flawless."
It is understandable that this song, especially verses 8-10, has
been a rich source of metaphors and titles used to honor the
mother of Jesus. In general those lines and songs in this book
which most clearly echo the mythology and cults of the fertility
religions are precisely the ones that have been utilized most
frequently by allegorical interpreters and mystics. This is only
natural, since the august language of the ancient cults lent itself
immediately to the religious purposes of the mystics.

The Nut Garden (6:11-12)

This little piece is difficult to interpret, chiefly because the
Hebrew of verse 12 is not well preserved. As it stands, it requires
us to understand that the lady is speaking, but many dispute this.
The scene in verse 11 is one of new life in nature, with budding
vines and pomegranates in bloom. Nut trees were a feature of
the garden of Adonis, the god of love and fertility, and we may
have an echo of that here. This descent to the garden is a symbol
to convey the message that spring, the time of love and new life,
has come.

The Dance of the Shulammite (6:13—7:10)

In Syria and in the Holy Land today the dance of the bride
climaxes the week-long wedding feast. It seems probable that this
song about the dance of the Shulammite maiden was set at a
similar point in wedding feasts in ancient Israel. It was used in
the celebration of a human social event. But its form and language again reflect ancient cultic rites.

The term "Shulammite" alludes to "Shalem," a Canaanite god
who seems to have been the patron deity of the pre-Israelite
city of Jerusalem (hence "Salem," Ps. 76:2). This Shalem, whose
name means completion or evening, was the twin of Shahar,
whose name means dawn or morning. Together they are the
morning and evening star and were patrons of love. Thus the
name "Shulammite" has cultic as well as royal connotations. In
the dance of the village bride there are echoes not only of
Solomon's queen but of an ancient god of Jerusalem.

But now, in a question probably sung by a chorus of women

(see 5:9; 6:1), it is asked how or "why" one should look upon the dancing Shulammite as upon one doing a war dance. "Mahanaim" (6:13, margin), a site east of the Jordan, literally means "two armies" or camps. According to tradition (Gen. 32:2), it was the place at which the angels who constituted the "army" of God had disclosed themselves to Jacob. Thus there were "two armies," Jacob's own force and the Lord's, to accomplish his return to Canaan. Hence what we have here is a reference to Israel's ancient institution of the "holy war" and to a sacred dance related to it. Not only the memories of Solomon and of the Canaanite deity for whom he was named but also those of the ancient war dance of Israel lived on in the songs of its later wedding feasts and in the title and dance of the bride.

The cry "Return" is a call to the bride to continue or repeat the dance, so that all may see her. The description of the dancer (7:1-5) begins with the "sandals" on her feet and ends with the "flowing locks" on her head. Its artistic form corresponds to descriptions already encountered (4:1-7; 5:10-16; 6:4-10). The intention is to create an impression about the dancer's personal qualities by the description of objects to which various parts of her body are compared; the body as such is not described. It is thus a rather subjective enterprise to try to recapture the impressions about his subject the singer sought to convey. Yet one is not left entirely to one's own imaginative devices, since many of the objects described occur frequently and have a clearly defined metaphorical meaning in Israel's poetry. Thus jewels made by a master craftsman (7:1) connote aesthetic perfection, bowls of wine and heaps of wheat imply plenty and, especially with "lilies" (7:2), fertility. Fawns are always quick and delicate (see 4:5a); towers are strong and stately, connoting self-possession (7:4). But whether the eyes are compared to "pools in Heshbon" because its waters are clear and pure, or because they sparkle, or because the pools are far away across the Jordan and not always in Israel's possession, who can say? On the other hand, the beauty and nobility of Mount Carmel were proverbial (7:5).

Having completed his step-by-step description of the dancing bride, the singer sums up his impressions in the oft-repeated adjectives "fair" and "pleasant." Taken as a whole she reminds him of the palm tree. The palm is tall, slender, and voluptuous. In the Temple, palms were symbols of vigor and fertility (Ps. 92:13-15; Ezek. 41:15-20). The "tree of life" in mythological traditions of the Near East, and subsequently in Israel and the Church, was pre-eminently the palm. One climbed the palm tree to gather its fruit. The song combines the theme of fruitfulness with highly erotic connotations.

The bridegroom has sung his song in honor of the dancing bride. Now (7:10) the bride sings a very simple and obvious response: I am his; his longing is for me.

Love in the Vineyard (7:11-13)

In this little song, as frequently, the bride invites her lover. Spring and the vineyard, budding vines and the pomegranate, have become established props for these songs. Vintage festivals in the autumn and the dance of the vineyards (Judges 21:16-24) were traditions that reached back to Canaanite times. The mandrake, whose fruit ripens "in the days of wheat harvest" (Gen. 30:14-16), in May, is still reckoned as an aphrodisiac in the Arab world. The bride has kept all her "choice fruits" of love until now, for her lover. In Christian tradition this song has been a great favorite, interpreted as the call of the Church to Christ.

The Bride's Yearning (8:1-4)

This is another song by the woman in love, not an invitation, as the preceding one, but a soliloquy. In ancient Israel, as in the Arab world today, a public display of affection between lovers is severely condemned. For a woman to flout custom in this matter is to forfeit her good name. This singer knows that well enough. If he were only my brother, she says; then "none would despise me" (8:1). But, difficult as it is for her in her eager mood, she will abide by the passive role the conventions prescribe for the bride.

In contrast to 3:4 where, after finding him by night, she brought him "into the chamber of her that conceived me," she cannot take such initiative here. If she could, she would give him her love, which is symbolized by "spiced wine" and pomegranate juice (vs. 2). Her picture of what would be is completed by including a stock allusion to sexual union also used in 2:6. Then, having imagined the consummation of their love, she repeats the oath exacted from the daughters of Jerusalem (2:7; 3:5; see also 5:8).

The Power of Love (8:5-7)

This little piece opens as a song, similar in form and spirit to all the rest of the book. But it closes on a reflective note reminiscent of the Book of Ecclesiastes. Riddle-like expositions of the strongest thing in the world were commonplace in contests to discover the man of greatest wisdom. An extensive account of such a contest is found in First Esdras. That particular contest was reportedly held before Darius, the Persian king, and the winner was Zerubbabel. He upheld the thesis that, while women were "stronger" than either the king or wine (the selections of his competitors), truth was strongest of all. The manner in which verse 7 here establishes the theme that nothing is stronger than love corresponds precisely with that employed in the account of the contest before Darius.

The question in verse 5 we may imagine as being sung by the "daughters of Jerusalem." In 3:6-11 there was a coming up from the wilderness of "the litter of Solomon." Here we have a picture of the couple walking, with the beloved leaning on her lover. Thanks to his love, he is content to walk thus encumbered.

In her exposition of love as the strongest thing in the world, the woman asserts that it is "strong as death." The Hebrew for the last of verse 6 is not clear. A possible translation of the last two lines would be: "Its flames are flames of fire, a thunderbolt of Yah" ("the Lord," as in "Hallelu*jah*"). The name of God occurs nowhere in the book; but the use of it in this poetic form would be quite in keeping with the character of the book and especially with the spirit of conviction that pervades this passage.

Other Suitors (8:8-10)

Largely because it seemed impossible to see any real meaning in it, this passage has served as the occasion for a good deal of sly humor. Although its interpretation can by no means be considered fully assured, there is a growing consensus about its meaning. The songs contain occasional hints (for example, 7:13) that the beloved preserves herself inviolate for her lover. This piece is best read as an account of other suitors and her persistence in refusal.

The speakers ("we") in verse 8 are probably the suitors, and the term "sister" is to be understood as the familiar synonym for bride. Their speech is really a bit of sarcastic humor; she has given them as little response as one might expect from a child who "has no breasts." The sarcasm deepens. Speaking as her patrons, they say: What would we do if ever one came along to ask for her hand? How can we prompt her to respond?

The next verse (vs. 9) must be read as a proposal to deal with this. What it seems to say is that they will quicken her interest with rich gifts: silver and cedar. The lady is thought of as a city with wall and gate whose surrender is sought by means of bribes, at the wall something for the wall and at the gate something for the gate.

Now, in verse 10, the lady responds, also in sarcastic vein. Far from lacking breasts and lacking desire, her "breasts were like towers" and they were protected as by a wall. And just because she coldly turns away all others, keeping herself inviolate for her lover, she is "in his eyes as one who finds peace" (see margin); that is, he wholly approves of her.

The Priceless Vineyard (8:11-12)

This is a "once upon a time" story. Solomon, the wealthy king, had a vineyard called "Baalhamon"; that is, possessor of wealth. It was held in fief by some of his nobles, from each of whom Solomon was due "a thousand pieces of silver" (see Isa. 7:23). Even so, their own proceeds still amounted to "two hundred." The lover tells this story; and the point of it, for him, is given in verse 12a: "My vineyard . . . is for myself." This vineyard is his beloved bride (vs. 12b; see 8:7b).

Call and Response (8:13-14)

The book closes with a call by the lover addressed to his beloved, who is said to be "in the gardens." With his wedding "companions," he wants to hear the voice of the bride (see 2:14). She replies, "Make haste," come quickly, and she completes her call in lines used elsewhere (2:17) of an invitation to the completion of their union. This conclusion is very probably also alluded to in the conclusion to the New Testament (Rev. 22:20) where the bride, which is the Church, answers to his promise that he is coming soon, "Amen. Come, Lord Jesus!"